LITTLE-KNOWN MUSEUMS

IN AND AROUND

LONDON

LITTLE-KNOWN

MUSEUMS

IN AND AROUND

LONDON

by Rachel Kaplan

HARRY N. ABRAMS, INC., PUBLISHERS

This book is for Kathy and Tana,
two women who have inspired and encouraged me every step of the way.

Editor: Adele Westbrook
Designer: Lorraine Ferguson

Library of Congress Cataloging-in-Publication Data
Kaplan, Rachel.
    Little-known museums in and around London / by Rachel Kaplan.
        p. cm.
    Includes bibliographical references and index.
    ISBN 0-8109-2699-7 (pbk.)
    1. Museums—England—London—Guidebooks. 2. London (England)—
    Guidebooks. I. Title.
    AM43.LSK36   1997
    069'.09421—dc21   96-52596

Front cover:
The western façade of Spencer House overlooking Green Park, London

Back cover:
The Student's Room, or Upper Drawing Office, at the Sir John Soane's
Museum, London

Rachel Kaplan was educated at the Lycée Français de New York, and at
Northwestern University, where she earned her B.S. in Journalism. She is an
international journalist who has written articles for American, British,
French, and Czech publications on a wide range of subjects. Her first book
was *Little-Known Museums In and Around Paris.*

Printed and bound in Hong Kong

 Harry N. Abrams, Inc.
100 Fifth Avenue
New York, N.Y. 10011
www.abramsbooks.com

CONTENTS

◆

Acknowledgments

◆

There are moments when the gods are truly on a writer's side. One of mine came, I believe, when I had the good fortune to meet Paul Gottlieb, President and Publisher of Harry N. Abrams, Inc. Not only did he give me wholehearted support for my first book, *Little-Known Museums In and Around Paris,* but he had the vision to see how this volume could be the first in a series that covered major capitals around the world, such as the volume you are holding in your hand, *Little-Known Museums In and Around London.* Moreover, I especially wish to thank my brilliant and committed editor, Adele Westbrook, whose careful and subtle editing, as well as superb organizational skills, have buoyed me throughout the creation of this book. My heartfelt appreciation also goes to Lorraine Ferguson, who not only devised this series' elegant and accessible design, but who knew how to beautifully integrate the text with the photographs so that they form a harmonious entity.

The artistry and passion that British photographer Nic Barlow brought to this project made it possible to reveal the many riches and surprises in these little-known museums—both inside and out. His knowledgeable recommendations concerning the selection of these museums, and his diligent assistance in working with these institutions, have added immeasurably to the content and value of this volume.

I would also like to thank the following museum curators and directors for their indispensable cooperation in the creation of this book: John Keyworth, Curator, Bank of England Museum; Anthony Burton, Director, Bethnal Green Museum of Childhood; Edward Bramah, Director, Bramah Tea & Coffee Museum; Sue Jackson, Director, Cabaret Mechanical Theatre; Dale Clarke, Creative Director, Clink Prison; Sophie Perkins, Curator, Cuming Museum; Stacey Pierson, Assistant Curator, Percival David Foundation of Chinese Art; Paul Thompson, Director, Penny Bassant, Public Relations Director, Design Museum; Dr. David Parker, Curator, Dickens House Museum; Richard Beresford, Curator, Lucy Till, Assistant Curator, Dulwich Picture Gallery; Francis Crosby, Deputy Head of Marketing & Public Relations, Duxford; Penny Hatfield, Archivist, Museum of Eton Life; Erica Davies, Director, Freud Museum; Rosemary Nicholson, Director, Rose Lea, Curator, Museum of Garden History; Christine Lalumia, Deputy Director, Geffrye Museum; Betty Gathergood, Curator, Dr. Johnson's House; Christina M. Gee, Curator, Keats House; Ian Dejardin, Curator, Kenwood House, The Iveagh Bequest; Michael Harrison, Director, Fiona Bond, Public Relations Director, Kettle's Yard; Julia Findlater, Curator, Leighton House Museum; Max Hebditch, Director, Jennifer Jones, Public Relations Director, Museum of London; Alex Attewell, Curator, Emma Buosi, Assistant Curator, Florence Nightingale Museum; Dennis Severs,

Director, Dennis Severs House; Helen Dorey, Deputy Curator, Sir John Soane's Museum; Stephen Jones, Director, Jane Rick, Curator, Spencer House; Margaret Benton, Director, Theatre Museum; Ken Flude, Director, Old St. Thomas's Operating Theatre, Museum, and Herb Garret; Rosamund Griffin, Keeper of the Collection, Waddesdon Manor; Rosalind Savill, Director, Wallace Collection; Valerie Warren, Curator, Wimbledon Lawn Tennis Museum.

On a more personal note, I would like to also thank my best friend and companion, Alexandre Bellas, for his loving patience and unflagging support.

—*R.K.*

Introduction

Encouraged by the success of *Little-Known Museums In and Around Paris* and the growing interest in museums off the beaten track, I wondered how many other European capitals might contain their own treasure troves of unusual and fascinating places that merited being better known. Several visits to London and its outskirts convinced me that a volume about museums in this great metropolis would yield its own pleasures and rewards. As it turned out, I discovered an embarrassment of undervisited riches. It is understandable why this is so: London alone boasts over three hundred museums and public galleries, making it the leading museum city in the world (a fact that often comes as a surprise to some of its own inhabitants).

Although Dr. Samuel Johnson defined the word "museum" in his *Dictionary* as "a repository of learned curiosities," the types of places I discovered while researching this book demonstrate how much the word's meaning has evolved since his time. Even Dr. Johnson might have been surprised to learn that there is a museum called Clink Prison, documenting the history of British incarceration until the end of the eighteenth century. Built on the foundations of the former prison and well-stocked with leg irons, gibbets, and other instruments of penal torture, it happens to be a popular locale for office Christmas parties! Just as unexpected was finding Old St. Thomas's Operating Theatre, Museum, and Herb Garret, located in the attic of a former church. This unique museum features an operating theater that was used until the 1860s, prior to the advent of anesthesia and antisepsis; its semicircular amphitheater from which the students used to observe gruesome operations taking place, and its crude wooden operating table, effectively conjure up a hapless patient's ordeal.

While most museum goers anticipate that their visits will be limited to an essentially visual experience, the London area features a number of places that challenge those assumptions. For instance, at the Museum of London you can hear the grunts and chirps of animals that once populated the British Isles during the Neolithic era, and caress stone flints and knives dating back 20,000 years; at Duxford, the largest aviation museum in Europe, you can fly in splendidly restored vintage aircraft; and at the Dennis Severs House in Spitalfields you are invited to partake in the domestic drama of a family of silk weavers, enhanced by a highly evocative usage of sights, sounds, and smells, ranging from the odors of freshly cooked roast beef and spilled punch, to the clip-clop of horses, the sudden shutting of doors and window sashes, and the steady, rhythmic pounding of machinery. (Because so many of these museums are atypical, it is advisable to call ahead to confirm visiting hours, as well as any special arrangements that might have to be made.)

The founders of these museums often seem as unique and as eccentric as the collections they amassed over a lifetime. While most of us know Sigmund Freud as the founder of psychoanalysis, few of us may realize that he spent much of his time and funds amassing an extraordinary collection of Egyptian, Greek, Roman, and Chinese antiquities (displayed at his home in Hampstead), and that he accorded as much importance to these ancient artifacts as to his pioneering work in mental health. Even more unusual was the architect Sir John Soane, who thought there was nothing out of the ordinary in exhibiting an Egyptian sarcophagus and a human skeleton in his basement, or the Cuming family, which collected just about anything, from the chocolate "stigmata" of Christ, which used to be sold in Paris during Easter Week, to the sawed-off leg of an Egyptian mummy.

If the London area has a fabulous cache of outstanding art collections, including those at the Dulwich Picture Gallery, Kenwood House, Kettle's Yard, Waddesdon Manor, and in the Wallace Collection, it is due in great measure to those discerning and enterprising collectors who knew how to profit from the fortuitous circumstances that enabled them to acquire quite a number of enviable masterpieces. With the current escalating art market, it is difficult to imagine that an individual family would have either the means or the opportunity to assemble a comparable collection today. The most notable case in point is that of the aesthete and art critic Jim Ede, who succeeded in acquiring the bulk of French sculptor Henri Gaudier-Brzeska's

estate in 1926 (now on display at Kettle's Yard) for all of sixty pounds!

Visiting these unique and varied museums not only provided a delightful way to learn numerous new things about England's rich and complex history (thanks largely to the museums' comprehensive educational materials), but also afforded me many unforgettable hours of pleasurable contemplation. Much of what I saw moved me profoundly, whether it was a few handwritten lines by the poet John Keats, a letter by the social reformer Florence Nightingale, or historical documents demonstrating how—well into this century—children were often forced to work and were thus deprived of schooling. In writing this book, I realized that each one of the museums I had come to know was a repository for one's respect, wonder, and admiration. In her book *A Natural History of Love,* Diane Ackerman writes: "Every museum is really a museum of one's high regard. . . . It functions as a sort of pilgrimage and vigil. We go there to express our love, our humility, our worship. Museums are where we store some of our favorite attitudes about life." It is my hope that the readers who accompany me in this happy discovery of *Little-Known Museums In and Around London,* even if it may be in the cozy comfort of their own living rooms, may come to share in this conviction.

Map of Museum Sites In and Around London

(see Numerical Legend on pages 14–15)

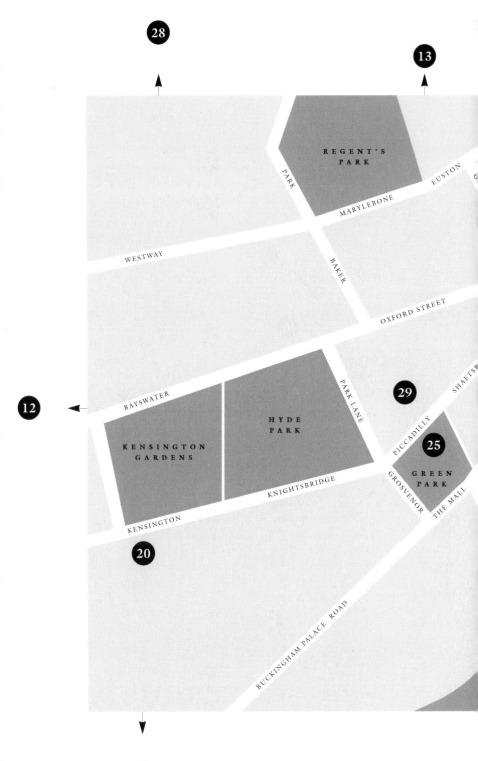

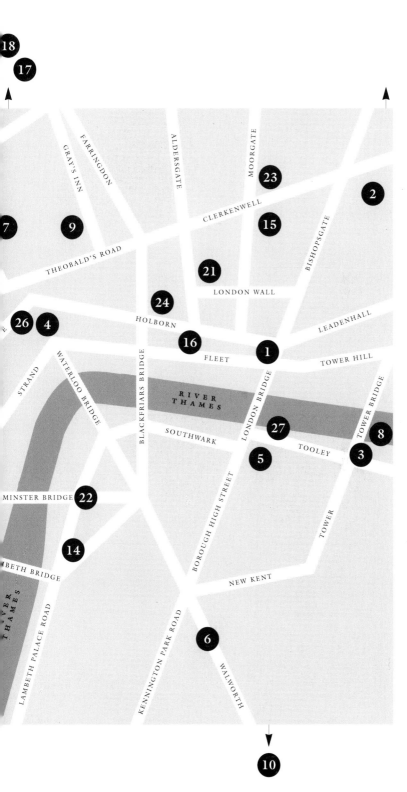

Numerical Legend for Museum Sites In and Around London

(see Map on pages 12–13)

1 Bank of England Museum

2 Bethnal Green Museum of Childhood

3 Bramah Tea & Coffee Museum

4 Cabaret Mechanical Theatre

5 Clink Prison

6 Cuming Museum

7 Percival David Foundation of Chinese Art

8 Design Museum

9 Dickens House Museum

10 Dulwich Picture Gallery

11 Duxford

12 Museum of Eton Life

13 Freud Museum

14 Museum of Garden History

15 Geffrye Museum

Bank of England Museum

Bartholomew Lane
London EC2R 8AH
Tel: 0171–601–4878

**Open Monday through Friday
10:00 A.M. to 5:00 P.M. except
holidays.**

Disabled Access.

**Underground: Take the Central
or Northern Line to Bank Station.
Bus: 8, D9, 11, 21, 22B, 23, 25,
26, 43, 133, 149**

ALTHOUGH paper money
was in use during the seventh century
in China, legal paper tender only
became widespread in Europe a
thousand years later. In the sixteenth
century, when London's goldsmith
bankers began to accept deposits,
make loans, and transfer funds for
their exclusive clientele, they also gave
redeemable receipts for the gold
coin deposited with them, known as
"running cash notes"—a forerunner
of modern bank notes.

IN 1694, THE BANK OF ENGLAND'S COURT OF DIRECTORS
CHOSE THIS IMAGE OF BRITANNIA AS THE BANK'S CORPORATE SEAL.
ORIGINALLY USED ON ROMAN COINS,
BRITANNIA SOON BECAME AN ACCEPTED DEVICE ON BRITISH BANK NOTES;
EVERY PRINTED NOTE ISSUED BY THE BANK CARRIES THIS SEAL.

THIS SPECIAL EXHIBIT ON THE HISTORY OF THE ONE-POUND NOTE IS PRESENTED
INSIDE THE RECONSTRUCTION OF A LATE-EIGHTEENTH-CENTURY BANKING HALL,
THE BANK STOCK OFFICE; THE ORIGINAL HALL, WHICH WAS BUILT BY SIR JOHN SOANE,
ENGLAND'S LEADING GEORGIAN ARCHITECT,
HAS BEEN COMPARED TO THE INTERIOR OF A BYZANTINE CHURCH.

In 1694, shortly after the Bank of England was created to raise money for King William III's costly military campaign against the French, the Bank began issuing notes in exchange for deposits that were redeemable in gold or coinage. These notes, which were issued for sums exceeding fifty pounds, were handwritten on the Bank's paper and signed by one of the cashiers. Relatively few people ever saw or used these notes from the Bank of England, however, which was hardly surprising, considering that the average income during this period was less than twenty pounds a year.

The fascinating history of the bank note is just one of the surprises awaiting visitors to the handsomely appointed Bank of England Museum, housed within the monumental Bank of England itself, in the heart of the City. Today, it is often taken for granted that the world's second oldest central bank (the Bank of Sweden was the first), much like the Federal Reserve in the United States, serves as bank to both the British government and to its banking system, and plays a key role in setting the monetary policy that affects the cost and availability of money and credit.

The visitor to this museum will be fascinated to learn that the Bank of England was the brainchild of a single Scottish financier, William Paterson, who proposed lending 1,200,000 pounds to the government at eight percent interest, in return for which the subscribers would be incorporated as a joint-stock company under the title "Bank of England." Once Parliament had approved this scheme, the loan capital was raised in less than two weeks as investors rushed to pour money into the new venture. The bank's original ledger book indicates that the first sums deposited ranged from as little as twenty-five pounds to as much as ten thousand pounds—the latter sum given in the names of King William III and Queen Mary.

After the Charter was signed on July 27, 1694, the Bank opened for business with a staff of seventeen clerks and two gatekeepers in temporary offices at the Mercers' Hall in Cheapside. Not until forty years after its founding did the Bank move to its present site on Threadneedle Street. George Sampson's new building, completed in 1734, is regarded as the first purpose-built bank in the world. It was quickly outgrown, however,

and single-story wings, in an elegant Palladian style were added by Sir Robert Taylor between 1765 and 1788. Taylor was succeeded as architect to the Bank by the greatest Georgian architect of the age, Sir John Soane, who held that post for forty-five years. During that time, the Bank was largely rebuilt in Soane's more austere classical style and extended to cover the present site. This structure, notable for its massive and seemingly impenetrable outer walls, remained unchanged until the 1930s, when the Bank's staff expansion necessitated a complete rebuilding. Under Sir Herbert Baker, Soane's single-story building was demolished (with the exception of the Bank's outer walls), and a new

THESE TWO NOTES REFLECT THE EVOLUTION OF BANK NOTES
SINCE THE EIGHTEENTH CENTURY:
AFTER 1725, THE BANK OF ENGLAND ISSUED PARTLY PRINTED NOTES
FOR COMPLETION IN MANUSCRIPT, SUCH AS THE ONE SHOWN ABOVE;
AFTER AN ABSENCE OF OVER A CENTURY
THIS BANK OF ENGLAND ONE-POUND NOTE WAS REINTRODUCED
(LATER KNOWN AS SERIES A).
THIS NOTE WAS THE FIRST COLORED NOTE AND THE FIRST TO
BE PRINTED ON BOTH SIDES BY THE BANK.

UNTIL THE INTRODUCTION OF
STEAM-DRIVEN PRESSES,
THIS MANUAL PRINTING PRESS
WAS WIDELY USED IN THE PRODUCTION
OF BANK NOTES.

THE ORIGINAL BANK CHARTER OF THE BANK OF ENGLAND BEARING
THE SEALS OF KING WILLIAM III WAS SIGNED ON JULY 27, 1694; SHORTLY AFTERWARD
THE BANK OPENED FOR BUSINESS AT THE MERCERS' HALL IN CHEAPSIDE.

seven-story building erected within, which was completed just before the outbreak of war in 1939.

Because the Bank is situated at the center of what was once Roman London (Londinium), the twentieth-century rebuilding program led to the discovery of extensive archaeological remains dating from the first to the third centuries, including a magnificent mosaic floor, part of which is now on display in the museum. Other items found on the site include a variety of iron styli, (writing instruments that were used to cut letters into wax tablets), bone hairpins, pottery, an early type of horseshoe, and even a leather sandal.

During the eighteenth century, the Bank developed as a government bank, with four-fifths of its business and profits resulting from its governmental connection. In addition to keeping the accounts of most departments of state, the Bank managed the entire national debt. This increased significantly as a result of the series of wars in which Britain was involved—from 12 million pounds in 1700 to 850 million pounds by the time Napoleon was defeated at Waterloo in 1815.

The Bank began issuing partially printed notes in 1725: the pound sign and first digit were printed, while other numerals were added by hand, as were the name of the payee, the cashier's signature, the date, and the number. By 1745, notes were being printed in denominations ranging from 20 to 1,000 pounds, the latter being equivalent to an estimated 68,000 pounds today. The first fully printed notes were issued in 1855, an event that brought relief to the Bank's team of cashiers, who no longer had to fill in the name of the payee and sign each note individually.

The forgery of bank notes has a history as old as the notes themselves. The first counterfeit note appeared only days after the Bank opened for business and anti-forgery devices, such as watermarked paper, were quickly introduced. After one forger was fined and pilloried for manufacturing sixty 100-pound notes, Parliament made counterfeiting a felony punishable by death or deportation to the colonies.

During the wars against France, the drain on the Bank's gold reserves led in 1797 to the suspension of the Bank's commitment to convert its notes into gold. To meet the shortage of circulating currency, the Bank issued one- and two-pound notes for the first time; prior to this, five-pound notes had been the lowest denomination. Forgers, like Charles Hibbert, whose wood and leather toolbox is displayed in the museum, were quick to profit from this situation. In 1801, the Bank introduced a waved line watermark in an effort to make its notes more secure, but many people were hanged for passing counterfeits, very often the innocent dupes of the forgers.

In 1819, the cartoonist George Cruikshank depicted their suffering on a mock bank note showing a mass gibbet and signed by "Jack Ketch," a popular nickname for the hangman. Such harsh sentencing was extremely unpopular, and a public campaign eventually succeeded in reducing the maximum sentence to life imprisonment. In 1855 the introduction of a watermark with degrees of shading, and the issue of fully printed, identical notes, helped to make notes more secure.

During World War II, in an effort to destabilize British sterling, the German government waged a major campaign to counterfeit British bank notes, some of which are on display in the museum. The notes were produced by inmates of the Sachsenhausen concentration camp as part of a large-scale forgery operation code-named "Operation Bernhard." By 1943 the German government was turning out some 500,000 counterfeit "British" notes a month. Fortunately,

most of these forged notes were not released, but were captured by the advancing Allied forces. Still, significant numbers did find their way into circulation and were a constant headache for the Bank and other financial institutions for years afterward. To counter the problem, the Bank introduced a metal thread for the first time, and in 1943 stopped issuing all denominations above five pounds. It was only between 1964 and 1981 that the ten, twenty, and fifty-pound denominations were reintroduced.

The museum's award-winning interactive video and software systems demonstrate just how far the Bank of England has come since its early days, when cashiers used up to five quill pens a day to sign bank notes and write down deposits in their voluminous ledger books. Two interactive computer systems allow visitors to look behind the doors of the nation's central bank, to see how its fast-paced dealing rooms have up-to-the-minute information on foreign exchange, gilt (government stock) and money markets, as well as to discover the intricacies of bank note design and production.

It gives one pause to learn that each year the Bank's Printing Works at Loughton in Essex produce nearly 1.4 billion notes (enough notes, put end to end, to stretch halfway to the moon), and that six tons of these used notes are crushed into fine particles every day before being buried in landfill. Clearly, the "Old Lady of Threadneedle Street" has come a very long way indeed.

THESE ENGRAVED METAL PLATES ARE USED
TO ADD THE PORTRAIT OF HER MAJESTY THE QUEEN
AND THE LETTERING ON THE FRONT OF THE BANK NOTE.
THIS PRINTING METHOD PRODUCES THE RAISED PRINT
THAT GIVE BANK OF ENGLAND NOTES THEIR
DISTINCTIVE FEEL.

Bethnal Green Museum of Childhood

Cambridge Heath Road
London E2 9PA
Tel: 0181-980-2415

Open Monday through Thursday
and on Saturday from 10:00 A.M.
to 5:50 P.M.; Sunday from 2:30
P.M. to 5:50 P.M.

Underground: Take the Central
Line to Bethnal Green.

IN the seventeenth and eighteenth centuries there was no such thing as a right or left foot for children's shoes, and the styles for girls and boys were virtually the same. Shoes were worn mainly by the wealthy, and until the nineteenth century, many children went barefoot. This lack of footwear was to have dire consequences for children's schooling—because the compulsory education law required that shoes be worn to school, poor parents, who couldn't afford them, had to keep their offspring at home.

This concise history of children's footwear, which is illustrated with rare examples of shoes, is just one of the many fascinating exhibits at the Bethnal Green Museum of Childhood, the only institution in Great Britain to document the life of children through the centuries.

The museum's brick and metallic structure is unique in itself, since it is among the world's oldest extant pre-fabricated buildings, having been erected in South Kensington in 1856 and then transferred to Bethnal Green in 1867 as a branch of the Victoria and Albert Museum. (The locale was initially used for temporary exhibitions, and later as display space for a rapidly expanding toy collection.)

When Sir Roy Strong became the Director of the Victoria and Albert Museum in 1974, it was decided that the Bethnal Green Museum should be dedicated entirely to childhood. Today, it boasts one of the world's largest public collections of toys, dolls, and games, reflecting the periods in which they were made. For instance, some displays demonstrate that after trains, automobiles, and

THIS BREATHTAKING VIEW OF THE BETHNAL GREEN MUSEUM—
LODGED INSIDE ONE OF THE OLDEST WROUGHT-IRON BUILDINGS IN GREAT BRITAIN—
REVEALS ONE OF THE WORLD'S LARGEST COLLECTIONS OF TOYS, DOLLS, AND GAMES.
THE MUSEUM'S FIRST CHILDREN'S TOY EXHIBITION WAS OPENED IN 1923,
WHICH SPURRED THE DEVELOPMENT OF A PERMANENT CHILDREN'S SECTION,
LATER ENLARGED UNDER THE PATRONAGE OF QUEEN MARY.
SINCE 1974, THE MUSEUM HAS CONCERNED ITSELF ENTIRELY WITH CHILDHOOD,
RECOUNTING ITS HISTORY THROUGH THINGS MADE FOR CHILDREN.

airplanes were invented, toy versions soon followed.

Yet the exhibits also show that many types of toys, such as board games, wooden spinning tops, dolls, lead soldiers, and stuffed animals have been reproduced generation after generation, often with little variation. Rather than present the development of toys chronologically, the curators have chosen to display the museum's vast holdings by type: dolls, dollhouses, teddy bears, trains, horses, and so forth. Some toys date as far back as the seventeenth century, such as a rare English doll and chair made of walnut (c. 1680) and an enchanting wooden dollhouse from

Nuremberg (c. 1673), once intended to instruct girls in the proper running of a household.

The museum also shows how the first mass-produced, hand-carved wooden toys were developed in the sixteenth century, primarily in Germany. Conditions for this industry proved particularly favorable: the country's supply of soft wood suitable for carving was plentiful, as was its water-based power supply, which drove the wood lathes. Moreover, there were many artisans from the Tyrol and Bavarian Alps who were willing to work for low pay, sitting for hours on end at long tables in wooden cottages, carving and painting toy

THIS APPEALING GERMAN CELLULOID DOLL HAS LOTS OF COMPANY, WITH EXAMPLES
DATING AS FAR BACK AS THE END OF THE SEVENTEENTH CENTURY.
THE DOLLS' DISPLAYS INCLUDE MATERIALS USED TO MAKE THEM: WOOD, COMPOSITION
OR PAPIER-MÂCHÉ, WAX, CERAMIC, CLOTH, AND PLASTIC.
WHILE SOME DOLLS WEAR GARMENTS NOTABLE FOR THEIR EXQUISITE NEEDLEWORK,
OTHERS ARE KEPT BARE TO SHOW THEIR BODY JOINTS.

parts before assembling them. Men tended to make wooden boats and games, whereas women fashioned wooden dolls. Then the toys were sent to Nuremberg and Leipzig, the industry's two major markets. German-made wooden toys proved so popular that, by the nineteenth century, they dominated the European market.

One of the most endearing exhibits is a collection of teddy bears, also called a "hug." Plush bear collectors or *arctophiles* (*arktos* in Greek means bear and *philos* means love) won't be disappointed: the museum contains every sort of stuffed bear imaginable, including Yorkshire cloth-covered bears stuffed with wood-wool (fine wooden shavings) or kapok, a softer, lighter, and more hygienic fiber, which comes from a tropical tree of the same name, as well as other hygienic and fireproof synthetic materials. There is even a 1908 teddy bear that growls when its head is tilted backwards!

The inspiration for the first teddy bear came from a cartoon published in a Washington, D.C., newspaper in 1902, showing the American president Theodore Roosevelt (whose favorite pastime was bear-hunting) refusing to kill a cub during a hunting expedition. A New York sweetshop owner, Morris Michton, seeing this cartoon, made a replica cub out of fabric, which he nicknamed "Teddy's Bear," and placed it alongside the cartoon in his store window. The bear became a huge overnight success (it was renamed the "teddy bear"), and soon Michton was mass-producing his stuffed plush toy. (The teddy bear became one of the best-selling items made by the Ideal Novelty & Toy Company that Michton founded in 1903, and which eventually became America's largest toy manufacturer.) Interestingly, the museum also notes that because German toy manufacturer Margaret Steiff began producing

THIS ANTIQUE MODEL CAR WITH ITS FEMALE "CHAUFFEUR" SHOWS HOW
TOYS OFTEN REFLECT THE TIME WHEN THEY WERE MADE;
WHEN TRAINS, CARS, AND PLANES WERE INVENTED, TOY VERSIONS SOON FOLLOWED.

stuffed bear cubs shortly after Michton, she claimed that she was the originator of the teddy bear.

Visitors are bound to be struck by the thoughtful and scholarly approach of the curatorial staff to the often overlooked history of children, bringing to life the experiences of a segment of society that has largely remained unseen and unheard. The museum's exhibits show that, until this century, children were extremely fortunate to reach adulthood. In eighteenth-century London, as many as seventy percent of the infants born each year died before the age of two, falling victim to an unbalanced diet and undernourishment. The extent to which people grieved for their lost children is borne out by an arresting seventeenth-century Iberian wax effigy of a dead child dressed in linen garments.

A display of child-feeding equipment includes some rare antique "pap boats" (an oval-shaped ceramic bowl with a lip at one end) for weaning and introducing infants to solid food, which were in use until the late nineteenth century. Pap was a mixture of flour or bread crumbs cooked in water or milk that was poured down an infant's throat. While this method of feeding may have improved the standards of cleanliness, it was not matched by an improvement in nutritional value.

The museum also shows how various forms of feeding and "sucking" bottles have been used since ancient times; a hollow cow's horn was one of the earliest forms of

SEVERAL EARLY EXAMPLES OF MASS-PRODUCED SOFT TOYS THAT
ONCE BELONGED TO THE CATTLEY FAMILY, WHO MADE CLOTHES FOR THEM,
PAINTED THEIR PORTRAITS IN WATERCOLOR,
AND TOOK THEIR PHOTOGRAPHS IN STUDIO-STYLE PORTRAITS
OR AT THE BEACH DURING A SEASIDE HOLIDAY.

artificial feeding receptacles, with widespread usage in Egypt, Western Europe, and Scandinavia. Pots with spouts at their center, called "bubby" pots were also employed from 3,000 B.C. onward; although they proved easier to administer, they were difficult to keep clean. Since the necessity of sterilizing milk and baby bottles was not understood until the end of the nineteenth century, "hand-raising" an infant from a bottle proved risky and could often result in death from infection.

Among the intriguing displays are late-eighteenth-century flat earthenware sucking bottles for babies, with stoppers in their middle to control the flow of liquid, and a glass or leather teat. Also on view are the first hand-blown glass baby bottles, which were produced in 1825.

It wasn't until the eighteenth century that previous assumptions about child rearing were challenged, primarily by the French educational reformer and philosopher Jean-Jacques Rousseau. He criticized the use of baby walkers, leading strings, caps, and padded hats that were meant to keep the heads of children warm, and claimed for the first time that children had rights of their own. His radical views ultimately paved the way for the introduction of legislation intended to protect children from economic and social abuse.

Among the most poignant exhibits is an 1810 employment contract indenturing a child apprentice to a weaver, illustrating the exploitation of children by employers and their own families. Besides performing chores referred to as "outwork" (such as making matchboxes at home), children were employed in mines, factories, and mills. In fact, the British textile industry was the largest employer of children in the nineteenth century.

Only the concerted efforts of social reformers and writers such as Charles Dickens succeeded in drawing attention to the terrible working conditions under which so many children labored, to the point where working hours for younger children were eventually reduced and Parliament passed a compulsory education act. Nonetheless, school attendance was often irregular. A Labor Permit for Leaving School shows that until 1900 a thirteen-year-old child could leave school and begin to work full-time. Not until 1972 was a law passed making schooling mandatory until the age of sixteen.

A visit to the fascinating Bethnal Green Museum of Childhood demonstrates that the history of childhood has had more than its share of growing pains. Still, the child in everyone can rejoice in the museum's wonderful collection of toys and games—those cherished playthings that have provided comfort and hours of pleasure to youngsters down through the centuries.

THESE RARE CHILDREN'S SHOES WERE ONCE WORN BY WELL-TO-DO BOYS AND GIRLS IN THE NINETEENTH CENTURY; A COTTON AND LEATHER PAIR (C. 1845), TOP LEFT, BELONGED TO PRINCE ALBERT EDWARD, THE ELDEST SON OF QUEEN VICTORIA.

THE BRAMAH TEAPOT IS THE LARGEST TEAPOT
EVER THROWN ON A WHEEL.
IT WAS COMMISSIONED BY EDWARD BRAMAH IN 1985
TO COMMEMORATE THE CENTENARY OF
THE HEIGHT OF THE TEA TRADE,
AND DEPICTS FAMOUS CHARACTERS AND IMAGES
ASSOCIATED WITH TEA.
THESE INCLUDE DARUMA, A BUDDHIST MONK
MENTIONED IN CHINESE TEA LEGENDS,
AND CATHERINE OF BRAGANZA, WIFE OF KING CHARLES II,
WHO HELPED MAKE THE BREW FASHIONABLE.
THIS POT, WHICH WAS MADE BY ALAN CAIGER-SMITH,
WOULD PRODUCE 800 CUPS IF IT WERE EVER USED!

Bramah Tea & Coffee Museum

The Clove Building
Maguire Street
London SE1 2NQ
Tel: 0171–378–0222

Open every day except Christmas
Day and Boxing Day 10:00 A.M.
to 6:00 P.M.

Underground: Take the Circle or
District Line to Tower Hill
Station, then walk over Tower
Bridge and down the steps to
Butler's Wharf, where signage is
posted indicating the museum.
Bus: 15 or 78 to Tower Hill or
the 42, 47, P11 to Tooley Street.

Tearoom and coffee bar.

OPPOSITE Tower Bridge and
the Tower of London, lies Butler's
Wharf, the dockside area where for
over 300 years tea and coffee, two of
the world's most important com-
modities, were unloaded from ships,
stored, and prepared for distribution.
In its heyday, Butler's Wharf handled
as many as 6,000 chests of tea a day.

That hectic hubbub of activity has
vanished from the Wharf, however,
which is now one of London's gen-
trified districts, known for its elegant
restaurants, upscale boutiques, and
avant-garde galleries. Nonetheless, the
rich history of the city's once-glorious
tea and coffee trade is kept very much
alive at the charming and fascinating
Bramah Tea & Coffee Museum.

THIS 1894 ADVERTISING POSTER FOR THE
UNITED KINGDOM TEA COMPANY PORTRAYS SAMUEL PEPYS,
THE FAMOUS SEVENTEENTH-CENTURY DIARIST,
WHO WROTE OF HIS FIRST CUP OF TEA, TAKEN IN 1660.
(THE POSTER ALSO LISTS THE THEN CURRENT
PRICES OF TEA.)

Open since 1992, it contains an exceptional collection of over 1,000 teapots spanning four centuries, strange-looking coffee machines, and a myriad of objects, ranging from tea chests to contemporary prints and engravings, illustrating how England, the first nation to popularize coffee in Europe, also became the world's largest tea importer.

This novel museum, located on the second floor of a boxy, white modern office building (a renovated spice warehouse), is the brainchild of Edward Bramah, whose career in tea and coffee began as a planter on a tea estate in Malawi in 1950. A professional teataster, an inventor of his own patented filtered-coffee machine, and the author of such books as *Novelty Teapots,* Bramah was uniquely qualified to undertake such a project.

"While tea is the beverage most associated with Great Britain, and which, in fact, did so much to alter the course of English history, very few people in this country know much about it, and the same can be said for coffee as well," he observes wryly. "Moreover, it's important to know both the 'old history' and the 'new history,' otherwise you may misunderstand the evolution of tea and coffee drinking entirely."

The museum's entertainingly informative exhibits and videos explain how the first coffeehouse was opened in Oxford in 1652. Originally, this exotic beverage was presented to a curious, yet wary public as having medicinal benefits—purveyors claiming that it "is a very good help for the digestion, quickens the spirit and is good against sore eyes." It wasn't long before the coffeehouse craze had caught on, attracting the patronage of such literary customers as Samuel Pepys, Joseph Addison, Daniel Defoe, John Dryden, and Oliver Goldsmith.

As they proliferated, coffeehouses began offering specific services to different types of clientele. In 1680, a private postal system (in violation of the official government monopoly) was devised to enable customers to use their regular coffeehouse as a place where they could both post and receive letters. Financial transactions were conducted so successfully at

Jonathan's in Exchange Alley that, by the following century, the coffeehouse had developed into the Stock Exchange. Merchants with an interest in shipping frequented the establishment owned by Edward Lloyd in Abchurch Lane. Twenty years after it first opened, it became not only the place where reliable information could be obtained, but also where ships could be insured. In 1769 a new Lloyd's Coffee House was established in Pope's Head Alley with membership strictly limited to those in the marine insurance business. From such modest beginnings, the world-renowned Lloyd's of London was born.

The museum, which contains displays of miniature tea bushes, as well as dried tea leaves in wooden tea chests, documents how the Dutch first brought tea to Europe via Java, from Macao, the Portuguese trading outpost on the Southern China coast. Exchanged for dry sage, tea arrived in Holland in 1610. "The Dutch made tea drinking the pinnacle of elegance, copying the Japanese and the Chinese," notes Bramah. "However, it would take Charles II and his wife, Catherine of Braganza, to make tea drinking fashionable in England."

Like coffee, tea was a social beverage. The museum's collection of period prints depicting scenes from the seventeenth and eighteenth-century tea and leisure gardens, shows how the stylish and the well-to-do in London frequented these spectacular covered gardens to drink tea, listen to music, and even watch fireworks displays. Mozart performed at one of the most successful—The Rotunda at Ranelagh—which featured a 150-foot rotunda resembling the Roman Pantheon.

As the coffeehouse declined, Britain evolved into a nation of tea

THIS DISPLAY OF CHINESE TEA CHESTS
SHOWS THE TYPES OF TEAS THAT
WERE ONCE AVAILABLE
AND HOW THEY WERE PACKED PRIOR TO
BEING SHIPPED FROM CHINA
TO ENGLAND.

drinkers, partly because the British East India Company held a monopoly on trade with China, the chief exporter of tea until 1850. (After the bitter outcome of the Chinese Opium Wars, the British established plantations in Ceylon and India, which eventually became the world's principal tea producers.) This evolution was furthered by the protection afforded to the sea routes by the Royal Navy, as well as by the fact that London enjoyed favorable docking and warehouse facilities. England's excellent network of canals and railways also played a vital role in the distribution of tea to the new factory and mill towns in the Midlands and in the North. Moreover, potteries at Stoke-on-Trent, and later at Spode, Newcastle-under-Lyme, and Bow, which developed both creamware and bone china, increased tea's popularity.

Bramah claims there is an inextricable link between the consumption of tea and the nation's Industrial

THE ITALIAN ESPRESSO MAKERS BY LA VICTORIA ARDUINO AND PAVONI
IN THIS DISPLAY DATE FROM THE EARLY TWENTIES.
THE MUSEUM FOLLOWS THE HISTORY OF ESPRESSO RIGHT THROUGH THE
GAGGIA MODELS INTRODUCED IN SOHO IN THE FIFTIES.

Revolution. "Factory owners discovered that tea, served with milk and sugar, was a stimulant, and that it both warmed the workers and improved their efficiency. And, unlike beer and gin, it kept people sober."

From the moment tea arrived in Great Britain, it was viewed as a valuable source of revenue by the Exchequer; by 1660 Charles II was granted the right to impose excise duties on the increasingly popular beverage.

From 1711 to 1810, the British state collected seventeen million pounds in taxes on tea, money that generated income to wage both the Napoleonic and Crimean Wars in the nineteenth century and the Boer and First World Wars in the twentieth. While import duty on tea was repealed temporarily in 1929 for three years, it wasn't until 1964 that the tea excise was finally abolished.

To avoid paying exorbitant import duties, the smuggling of tea became a highly organized national enterprise, to the extent that, in the eighteenth century, almost two-thirds of the tea trade consisted of bootlegged product. It would take the Commutation Act of 1784 under Prime Minister William Pitt to cut taxation from 119 percent to 12.5 percent, thus putting the smugglers out of business.

According to Bramah, the modern era of tea and coffee drinking in the British Isles began in the early 1950s. Tea remained rationed until 1956, four years after the espresso machine was introduced in London and the coffee bar came into vogue. Still, while coffee had become the second largest trading commodity in the world after oil, in Great Britain it had barely a two-percent market penetration at the time. "The problem for the coffee-producing countries was how to persuade the British to make coffee when they were happy drinking

tea," Bramah notes. "Nestlé and General Foods chose to overcome this problem by introducing coffee as a soluble powder, rather like cocoa. As luck would have it, in 1956 British television began running commercials. Were it not for television advertising, which has promoted instant coffee almost every night since 1956, it is doubtful that even this instant product would have succeeded."

The tea trade responded to this challenge that threatened its virtual monopoly by asking tea producers in India and Africa to cultivate a tea that would infuse more quickly. After centuries of drinking slow-infusing tea, the magic words of copywriting ("Quick Brew," "Super Brew," "Fast Brew") persuaded tradition-bound tea drinkers to switch to the tea bag, which now accounts for seventy percent of tea sales in the United Kingdom. (Today, forty percent of the British public drinks coffee, while the other sixty percent prefers tea.)

Purists at heart, the staff at the Bramah Tea & Coffee Museum have strong reservations about most quick-infusing teas and tea bags, accusing them of making "an extraordinary red color in the cup, the teapot and the sink!" Still, even if differences of opinion over tea may persist, visitors to this intriguing museum are bound to concur with a motto painted on one of its German porcelain teapots:

In far away lands, or wherever you be
Friendship is welded by a good cup of tea.

Cabaret Mechanical Theatre

33/34 The Market
Covent Garden
London WC2E 8RE
Tel: 0171–379–7961

**Open Monday through Saturday
10:00 A.M. to 6:30 P.M.;
Sunday 11:00 A.M. to 6:30 P.M.**

**Underground: Take the Piccadilly
Line to Covent Garden Station.
Bus: 6, 9, 11, 13, 15, 77A, 170,
176, 196**

IN PAUL SPOONER'S VERSION OF
TIPOO'S TIGER, THE CAPTION ASKS:
"IS THE GLOATER UNABLE TO
IMAGINE HIMSELF
IN THE VICTIM'S PLACE OR IS IT FROM
JUST SUCH IMAGININGS
THAT HE GETS HIS PLEASURE?"

T H I S may be the only place in
London where you can have your
hand "cut off " by the *Great
Chopandoff,* test your nerves against
a *Rabid Dog,* or get the fright of your
life from *Crankenstein,* a monster that
even Dr. Frankenstein would have
appreciated.

Step right into the Cabaret
Mechanical Theatre, Great Britain's
most intriguing collection of contemporary automata, located in the heart
of Covent Garden within a cave-like
gallery whose atmosphere is regularly
punctuated by the sounds of delighted squeals and cries of surprise. After
visitors purchase a ticket, a handmade, life-size wooden mechanical
man stamps it, and the theatre's doors
fly open to reveal an exhibition of
sixty-four handmade automata that
can be brought to life by a mere
touch of a button. Adding to the
overall pandemonium is a nineteenth-
century nickelodeon piano that plays
sentimental cabaret music continuously—a fitting backdrop for the
colorful, witty, and comical automata
on display.

The impishly clever "impresario"
behind Cabaret Mechanical Theatre
is Sue Jackson, who first came across
such wooden automata when she
was running a tiny craft shop in
Falmouth, Cornwall, which sold
everything from wooden toys to
hand-knitted sweaters. Enchanted
with the brightly colored wooden
moving constructions made by her
friends Peter Markey and Paul
Spooner, she soon began a collection
and used them as eye-catching window displays in her shop. She became
acquainted with other artists,

cultivating, encouraging, and inspiring them—including Richard Windley, Michael Howard, Ron Fuller, and Tim Hunkin. Eventually, her shop became crammed with a considerable assortment of automata that were not for sale. Customers could look and even touch, but they couldn't buy.

As a business venture, this system clearly had its drawbacks. Would people, Sue Jackson wondered, be prepared to pay ten pence to see an automaton spring to life? There was only one way to find out. After installing Spooner's most elaborate coin-operated automaton depicting a skeleton titled *The Last Judgement*, Jackson and Spooner went off to the pub. Returning some time later, they discovered five pounds in ten pence pieces in the machine! What had seemed like a mere device, now struck them as a brilliant idea. The principle had worked. Moreover, by dividing the receipts between the shop and the artist, this method could be used to provide a regular and continuing income for both. This rule still applies to any money inserted in the coin-operated automata at the Cabaret Mechanical Theatre.

"The best part of this arrangement was that now I had a good excuse for keeping the automata," Jackson explains. "And it was a way in which I could generate enough income to continue commissioning and showing more work." While works by Spooner, Hunkin, Markey, Fuller, and Howard form the heart of the collection, other automatists present themselves from time to time. Recent discoveries include Keith Newstead, noted for his striking brass mechanical automata, such as an aluminum peacock whose metallic plumage opens into a dazzling fan, and his witty aluminum *Jukas Giles Agriplane* that is "fueled" by whiskey

"I'D LIKE TO BE UNDER THE SEA" BY KEITH NEWSTEAD IS A WITTY HOMAGE TO THE BEATLES' SONG.

PAUL SPOONER'S UPRIGHT *BANE CAT* IS JUST ONE OF A SERIES OF UNSETTLING YET ENTERTAINING FELINES THAT POPULATE HIS PERSONAL MYTHOLOGY.

and whose livestock cargo consists of a metallic pig.

For the uninitiated, the Cabaret Mechanical Theatre provides "an unreliable history of automatons" that is almost as compelling as the collection itself. Automatons, (the word comes from the Greek *automatos* meaning "acting of itself") have been around since 2,000 B.C., when the Egyptians placed them in their tombs. These were mainly simple working models of tradesmen who might be useful to the deceased in the afterlife.

The Greeks were also fond of these types of mechanisms, and in the second century the mathematician Hero of Alexandria used automata as demonstration models for his treatises on pneumatics, hydraulics, and mechanics. These included a simple warbling bird and a highly elaborate automaton of Hercules and a dragon.

Leonardo da Vinci, whose notebooks contain drawings of automata (including flying machines), created a mechanical lion that greeted the French King Louis XII as he entered Milan. Apparently, the life-size lion walked towards him, stopped, and opened its chest to reveal the *fleur-*

de-lis, the French coat of arms. Similarly, in the seventeenth century, the French philosopher and mathematician René Descartes built a female automaton he called *"ma fille Francine."* Unfortunately, her life came to an unexpectedly brutal end during a sea voyage. Without Descartes' knowledge, the ship's captain opened the case containing Francine and, on seeing her move, assumed that she must have been the work of the Devil and threw her overboard!

One of the most extraordinary automata of the eighteenth century was the famous *Tipoo's Tiger.* Made for Tipoo Sultan, the ruler of Mysore, it depicts a European soldier being mauled to death by a tiger. While its movements are limited, it embodies a type of organ that reproduces the sound of a tiger's roar and a man's screams. This automaton was taken by the British after the defeat and death of Tipoo in 1799, and is now in the Victoria and Albert Museum.

Paul Spooner, who has contributed more pieces to Cabaret than any other automatist—forty-five at last count—has built his own highly personal version of *Tipoo's Tiger,* showing a humorous painted wooden tiger sporting an umbrella and chewing on the remains of his human dinner. The caption beneath the automaton reads, in part: "Our small tableau draws a veil over the disturbing meat course and shows the mighty diner extracting the last vestiges of flavor from his victim's braces. One of the nastiest human traits is to gloat over the suffering of others. Is the gloater unable to imagine himself in the victim's place or is it from just such imaginings that he gets his pleasure?"

Spooner likes to put his own disconcerting spin on such famous works of art as Edouard Manet's *Olympia* and Hieronymus Bosch's *The Last Judgement*. He also has developed his own personal mythology around Anubis, "the Egyptian jackal God of the mummy wrappings" and features this mordantly wry figure in many of his pieces.

Perhaps the most "philosophical" of the craftsmen represented in Cabaret, Spooner maintains a love/hate relationship with machines, finding people's confidence in technology touchingly absurd. Yet, at the same time, he is keen to show the mechanisms that empower his works. Despite the tremendous attention to detail and the exquisite carving that characterize his pieces, Spooner tends to deprecate his work: "You can pretend that making automata is a sensible activity, like digging for coal, but I actually think it's a neurotic act. You make models of a hypothetical world in order to have to avoid dealing with the real one."

The work of Tim Hunkin, on the other hand (whose life-size automata are consciously populist), can be likened to three-dimensional cartoons, which poke healthy fun at society. Most of his creations, including *The Doctor, The Barman, The Oracle,* and *Test Your Nerve,* are coin-operated and involve some degree of audience participation—very often they deliver a hefty "punch line."

About his works, Hunkin comments: "I used to have great trouble wondering what was the point of making anything until I started making slot machines. It's very satisfying hearing people laugh and scream at things I've made. Also, it's very satisfying emptying out the money. Conventional sculpture now seems rather dull in comparison."

In an increasingly homogeneous and mass-produced world, the Cabaret Mechanical Theatre remains a haven of wit, creativity, and individuality that occupies the strange and continuously shifting worlds of art, craft, and business. Visitors are constantly asking why they can't buy the automata in the exhibition. Jackson's answer is simple: "If someone buys a piece, they take it home with them and only they and their immediate friends can enjoy it. If it stays here, thousands of people can enjoy it every year." It's nice to know that principle and pleasure are able to successfully co-exist at this amusingly eccentric and enchanting museum.

ONE OF THE CLINK'S JAILERS, OR "KEEPERS,"
STANDS READY TO CHAIN AND CONFINE A PRISONER
TO THIS TORTURE CHAIR.
KEEPERS, WHO WERE OFTEN GIVEN SUCH A JOB INSTEAD OF A PENSION,
WERE POORLY PAID AND MANY SUPPLEMENTED THEIR INCOMES
BY EXTORTING VARIOUS PAYMENTS
FROM PRISONERS AND THEIR FAMILIES.

Clink Prison

1 Clink Street
London SE1 9DG
Tel: 0171-403-6515

Open every day
10:00 A.M. to 6:00 P.M.

Underground: Take the Northern
Line to London Bridge, then
follow the signs to Southwark
Cathedral and Clink Prison.
Bus: 17, 21, 22A, 35, 40, 43, 44,
47, 48, 95, 133, 149, 214, 501,
505, 513

First, descend a flight of stairs, stopping by the barred doorway of the Keeper of the Gate, whose job it once was to make sure convicts paid for their imprisonment. (Nowadays, one gets off easy by paying only for the tour.) Through a medieval archway looms the wax figure of a woman in rags chained to a grate, begging for alms. In the reconstructed guardhouse, a heavily armed figure dressed as a soldier in medieval garb, manacles a prisoner. Next door is the forge, where manacles were made and fitted. In the reconstructed prison ward—an appropriately dark and gloomy interior, furnished with chains and stocks from the period—visitors listen to the re-enacted plight of a young female prisoner who has been condemned to a wretched cell while waiting for her case to come to trial.

Welcome to Clink Prison—"the prison that gave its name to all others"—housed in a former warehouse built on the very foundations of the original prison, where visitors can learn about the history of penal conditions in Southwark from the fifteenth century through the eighteenth century. (A fragment of the original prison's walls, uncovered during the museum's construction, is featured in the exhibit.)

Inspired by a late fifteenth-century description of Marshalsea Prison (where Charles Dickens's father was imprisoned for debt), Clink Prison also presents the colorful history of the Thames's Bankside area, the land once owned by the Bishops of Winchester, notorious for its licensed "stewes," or brothels, which provided successive generations of clerics with lucrative incomes for almost five hundred years. By the seventeenth century, the brothels were just one highlight of a district that offered every kind of pleasure and entertainment, including bull- and bear-baiting, theaters, bowling alleys, and gambling dens.

The Bishop's manor—known as a "Liberty" because it was under canonic or Church law—had its own court (which dealt with everyday offenses ranging from prostitution to thievery, as well as religious dissent and debt) and its own prison (the Clink), where men and women were incarcerated together by the end of the fifteenth century.

While historians have speculated that the name "Clink" comes from the old Anglo-Saxon word meaning "to clench" or from the "clinking" of chains, it is more likely that it has its origins in Old Dutch, the language spoken by the Flemish community, which ran many of the Bankside brothels. (*Klink* in Old Dutch, as well as in modern Afrikaans, is the word for jail.)

Until the nineteenth century, prisoners were expected to pay for their imprisonment, since it was something that they had brought upon themselves. Those who could, depended on family or friends; those with a trade were often permitted to practice it (including prostitution). Others survived mainly thanks to alms and to begging through a barred window—although sometimes in the streets, attached to a ball and chain.

Because jailers were poorly paid, they often supplemented their income by exacting various forms of payment from the prisoners and their families. Fees were charged for everything

THESE TWO DIFFERENT TYPES
OF LEG IRONS ENSURED THAT NO PRISONER
WOULD EASILY ESCAPE.

from food and drink to fuel and clothing. Prisoners also paid a fee for entering and leaving jail, as well as for fitting and removing their fetters and irons. The keepers' corrupt practices could sometimes be used to the prisoner's advantage. For instance, in 1618 the Clink's warden was accused of willful negligence and corruption after allowing Catholic priests in his charge to say Mass in Latin and travel outside the prison.

Despite the exhibits of gibbets, stocks, and other gruesome features of incarceration, Clink Prison's current creative director, Dale Clarke, maintains that the purpose of this museum is to "tell a story, even though the story may be shocking." While male and female prisoners tended to share the same prison wards, they were not subjected to the same punishments. Only men were hanged, or drawn and quartered, whereas women were either drowned or burned at the stake. (Execution by burning was removed from the statute books only in 1790.)

Some of the punishments endured by women reveal their subjugated roles: for instance, those who were viewed as scolds were tied to "ducking stools," which were then dunked into the Thames—a punishment that stopped just short of drowning. Women who could not keep a "still and civil tongue" were locked into a scold's bridle, or "brank," which prevented speech by means of an iron plate that depressed the tongue. During the Commonwealth period, following the English Civil War, prostitution was suppressed, and any woman convicted of harlotry was branded on the forehead with a *B* for *bawd*.

When Henry VIII became head of the Church of England, he decreed that any disagreement with the teachings of that Church was tantamount to treason. During the reigns of the Tudor monarchs, and the Stuarts who followed them, the Clink Prison contained an unusual mixture of Catholic "Recusants," Protestant "Puritans," and common criminals. The Protestants were seldom as well connected or as wealthy as the Catholics, and seem by all accounts to have suffered greater hardships while incarcerated.

One of the Clink's best-known dissenters was Father William Weston, a Catholic priest imprisoned between September 1586 and January 1588, who gave an account of his ordeal in his memoirs *Midnight at the Clink*. A wax figure of Weston preparing for a clandestine Mass, allows visitors to imagine how he hid his silver Communion set beneath the prison's floorboards out of the wardens' sight. According to Weston's account, the dissenters' religious fervor was such, that even some of the Clink's jailers were converted. "Nevertheless, with all the tribulations, persecution and even death which the Catholics suffered daily, three of our keeper's own family were converted to the faith, also an assistant warder; one very old man and a young girl who left her former employment and henceforth gave devoted service to Catholic masters," he wrote.

Two brilliant Protestant theologians, John Greenwood, a clergyman, and Henry Barrowe, a lawyer, were imprisoned in 1586 and held in the Clink for six years before being granted unofficial parole. While they were incarcerated, Greenwood and Barrowe wrote two books, which were smuggled out a page at a time by a servant girl for publication in Holland. The English Ambassador to Holland sent a clergyman, Francis Johnson, to buy up and destroy all their written works. However, Johnson was so impressed by these two theologians that he converted to their faith, and eventually was himself imprisoned in the Clink!

After the execution of Greenwood and Barrowe at Tyburn in 1593, Johnson became a pastor of the Southwark Independent Church, and petitioned Elizabeth I for permission to emigrate to America. Finally, in 1620, a Southwark contingent from the Clink was able to join a large group of religious dissenters aboard the *Mayflower* and *Speedwell* ships and start a new life in the British Colonies.

However, for many ex-convicts, Puritans or otherwise, the trip to America was anything but a ticket to freedom. According to E. J. Burford's *A Short History of the Clink Prison*, "it became Government policy to supply the planters with willing 'slave labor.' This created a very lucrative racket in the City for shipping 'convicts' to the slave-owners in the colonies. Many thousands were shipped, including prostitutes from the Clink, many of whom became settlers' wives and Mothers of the American Revolution."

After the Great Fire of London in 1666, city merchants and developers flooded into Southwark, steadily displacing the old riverside inns and

THIS EIGHTEENTH-CENTURY ENGRAVING
DEMONSTRATES THE BRUTAL TREATMENT TO WHICH
PRISONERS COULD BE SUBJECTED,
FROM BEING STRIPPED OF THEIR BELONGINGS
TO BEING WHIPPED.

brothels that provided the Clink with its prisoners. The prison's end finally came in 1780 with the eruption of the anti-Popery riots in London. In keeping with a time-honored tradition, the rioters burned down the Clink Prison and all other premises on Clink Street, with the exception of the brewery, which was saved by the quick-wittedness of the brewer, who served the rioters meat and ale until the troops arrived and dispersed them. The prison was never rebuilt and the site was eventually cleared for factories and warehouses.

"You can judge the state of a civilization from the way it treats its criminals," notes Clarke. "We try to bring home to people that if you didn't pay your bills over two hundred years ago, this is the kind of place and fate you could expect. Our aim is to show visitors how things were done and let them draw their own conclusions." Moving through this museum devoted to the history of incarceration, no one can dispute that a visit to Clink Prison provides a unique vision of London and its past.

Cuming Museum

The Museum of Southwark's
History
155–157 Walworth Road
London SE17 1RS
Tel: 0171–701–1342

Open Tuesday through Saturday
10:00 A.M. to 5:00 P.M.

Underground: Take the Bakerloo
Line to Elephant & Castle,
then take the 12 or 171 Bus to
Walworth Road, getting off at
Walworth Library.

AN ancient mummified leg sawed off an Egyptian mummy. A framed patch of silk from the waistcoat of Charles I. Stucco chips taken from the room where Napoleon died on the island of Saint Helena. An eighteenth-century astrological cup from Sri Lanka made of coconut and carved with the signs of the zodiac. A petrified human scalp from North America, which was kept as a victory trophy. A pair of tiny embroidered silk Chinese slippers worn by a woman with bound, mutilated feet the size of a one-year-old child's.

All of these items represent merely a fraction of the things that visitors will discover at the highly unusual Cuming Museum, home to the collection of two remarkable British gentlemen, Richard Cuming (1777–1870) and his son Henry Syer Cuming (1817–1902), who dedicated their lives and fortune to assembling a startling array of bizarre and one-of-a-kind objects from all over the world documenting humanity's development since Antiquity.

When Henry Cuming died, he left over 100,000 labeled and catalogued objects, and enough money to build a museum in which to display them. Opened in 1906, the museum was advertised as "a British Museum in miniature." This was no overstatement, considering the size of the exhibition space (a single second-floor gallery) and the extraordinary variety and rarity of the collections, which cover such diverse fields as natural history, geology, archaeology, ethnography, ceramics, and the decorative arts. Although the museum has undergone significant

HENRY CUMING'S RECONSTRUCTED OFFICE REVEALS THE PREDILECTIONS
OF A VICTORIAN GENTLEMAN COLLECTOR AND AMATEUR SCIENTIST—
NOTE THE STUFFED FISH ON HIS DESK
AND THE STUFFED MONKEY NEXT TO THE CHAIR.

changes since it first opened, it continues to maintain the Cumings' labeling and system of classification, with the collections divided into "natural and artificial curios."

It is easy to get the impression that these two maverick collectors considered *everything* to be interesting, from an ancient Egyptian canopic jar that once held the lungs of a mummy, to such mundane objects as a cigarette butt smoked and discarded by a member of the Royal family. In planning his museum, Henry Cuming wrote that his intention was to "create a storehouse of knowledge for the merchant and manufacturer, for the archaeologist and the historian; the painter and the dramatist, for the military and naval tactician; for the philanthropist and philosopher; for

the lover of general knowledge." He would be happy to know that to this day leading scholars and researchers from around the world make special trips to visit his museum to study different parts of the collection.

"Both men were persuaded that the more they collected, the more they would know," notes curator Sophie Perkins. "They also believed that the more people knew of the past and other cultures, the more they would be able to demonstrate that the Victorian Age represented the pinnacle of progress."

The Cumings' determination to prove that the nineteenth-century Englishman was a superior being compelled them to be among the first ethnographers to collect and display Persian and Turkish slippers, as well

THESE FAKE "MEDIEVAL" STATUETTES MADE OF LEAD,
KNOWN AS "BILLY AND CHARLEYS,"
WERE SOLD IN THE MID-NINETEENTH CENTURY
AS TREASURES FROM A RECENTLY DISCOVERED CIVILIZATION.
HENRY SYER CUMING COLLECTED THEM,
KNOWING FULL WELL THAT THEY WERE FAKES.

as circular playing cards, African necklaces made of glass and bone beads, animal teeth, iron rings and spirals, bracelets made of giraffe's hair, unusual Chinese instruments, such as a mouth organ composed of seventeen bamboo reeds—even a gourd bottle from the Sandwich Islands brought back by the noted explorer Captain James Cook.

Richard Cuming's passion for collecting was first awakened when his aunt gave him a present of three fossils and an old Indian Mughal coin for his fifth birthday. He became a noted amateur scientist (the museum displays a telescope he built at fifteen), who lectured widely on such diverse topics as mechanics, chemistry, optics, and electricity, and who enhanced his collections by buying from other museums and explorers. Among his notable acquisitions were early Etruscan pottery and terracotta figurines purchased from the Prince of Canino, and rare Egyptian artifacts bought from such pioneering Egyptologists as James Burton, Sir Henry Salt, and Giovanni Baptista Belzoni (the latter, a former circus strongman turned adventurer, pillaged many sites, including the Valley of the Kings at Luxor).

"This type of collection could never be built today, because it goes against international law," notes Perkins. "In the nineteenth century Egyptian and Etruscan objects were plundered indiscriminately. It's hard to imagine that people would ransack tombs, remove mummies, unwrap them and cut them up into parts that were later sold off. That's how Cuming got a mummified leg. When people couldn't afford to buy a whole mummy, they contented themselves with a piece of one."

Like his father, Henry Cuming continued to collect from all over the world, particularly everyday objects

WHEN THE CUMING MUSEUM OPENED IN 1906, IT WAS DESCRIBED AS A "BRITISH MUSEUM IN MINIATURE," DUE TO ITS UNIQUE COLLECTION OF ORDINARY AND EXTRAORDINARY OBJECTS. THE MUSEUM'S COLLECTION OF LOCAL OBJECTS ILLUSTRATES SOUTHWARK'S DEVELOPMENT FROM AN AREA RENOWNED FOR THEATRICAL ENTERTAINMENT TO A THRIVING BOROUGH OF SOUTH LONDON.

used by peoples in the Americas, the Caribbean, Africa, the Near East, and Southeast Asia. Nor did he stop there. As vice-president of the British Archaeological Association, he had an inordinate interest in the archaeology of Southwark and London. Before excavations were being conducted scientifically, he was amassing thousands of historic objects dug up during the vast rebuilding of the city, including part of the famous "Battersea Treasure" of rare Anglo-

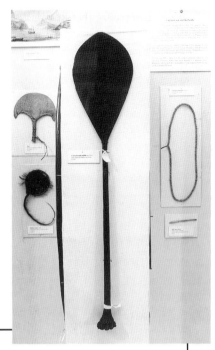

Saxon artifacts now in the British Museum.

Among the museum's remarkable domestic objects are a Roman toy (c. A.D. 100–300), a Roman figure of Venus from the same period, Roman keys, fragments of iron and brass chain mail from the fourteenth century, a pewter boatswain whistle and a pewter sacramental cruet from the fifteenth century, steel shears from the sixteenth century, and a seventeenth-century carved apple scooper made from a sheep's shank bone.

The Victorians' thirst for accumulating antiquities generated a lucrative market for fakes, many of which were sold to gullible collectors. Few understood this situation as well as Henry Syer Cuming, who had a pivotal role in exposing the notorious "Billy and Charley" fraud. Two East Enders, William Smith ("Billy") and Charles Eaton ("Charley"), who worked as mudlarks searching the banks of the Thames for valuable finds, eventually concluded that it would be far more profitable to cast their found objects in lead and bathe them in acid that simulated aging. Their extensive output consisted of "medieval" medallions, statuettes (mainly of knights and kings), daggers, and earthenware flasks, which in some instances were incised with jumbled words that made no sense. This was hardly surprising, since neither forger was literate.

Although the two forgers insisted their "medieval" artifacts had been uncovered in Shadwell, where a new dock was being built, Cuming's suspicions were aroused when a great number of these so-called "finds" suddenly began flooding the market. (As many as five or six of these fakes were being made each day.) Because he himself was a knowing collector of fakes (one of the museum's prize fakes is a so-called "Roman cinerary jar" made from an anchovy bottle filled with sand and rubbish), Cuming dared to challenge the authenticity of the Shadwell "discoveries" in print, an action that prompted the antique dealer who traded in these "medieval" objects to sue for libel. Although the case's outcome proved inconclusive, an amateur sleuth eventually succeeded in bribing another mudlark to break into the forgers' workshop and steal their molds, which were then exhibited at the Society of Antiquities in London. Still, not even this action put a stop to these counterfeiters. Not only were they never prosecuted, but both continued selling thousands more fakes to other unsuspecting collectors!

Although the bulk of the collections were assembled by the

Cumings, visitors shouldn't overlook the exhibits devoted to local Southwark history nor Edward Lovett's novel array of forgotten popular customs and superstitions presented to the museum in 1916. Coral necklaces worn by children to ward off sore throats, "fairy" or adder beads made from a fossil called zoophyte to protect against witchcraft and nightmares, and copper coins with holes in them worn as charms to ensure wealth, are among the many interesting items on view.

The diversity of the Cuming Museum may strike visitors as distinctly unorthodox. However, it is important to realize that its collections were compiled at a time when educated people were trying to understand the past and the world around them. "By collecting 'real' things the Cumings helped to initiate this discovery and reordering of the world—an ordering which continues to inform our way of thinking today," notes Perkins. "These collections are given their coherence by the theme of discovery. Hopefully, they permit our current visitors to enjoy the past and the wider world with the same enthusiasm as that displayed by the Cumings."

THIS MILK CART WAS USED
BY J.E. ROWLING TO SELL MILK IN THE STREETS
OF SOUTHWARK (C. 1900).

Percival David Foundation of Chinese Art

53 Gordon Square
London WC1H OPD
Tel: 0171-387-3909

Open Monday through Friday
10:30 A.M. to 5:00 P.M.

Underground: Take the Circle,
Metropolitan, or Hammersmith
& City Line to Euston Square
or the Piccadilly Line to
Russell Square.
Bus: 7, 8, 10, 14, 18, 19, 24,
25, 27, 29, 30, 38, 55, 68, 73,
91, 98, 134, 135, 168, 176,
188, 253

SINCE 1952, THE PERCIVAL DAVID
FOUNDATION OF CHINESE ART
HAS BEEN INSTALLED IN A CONVERTED
TOWN HOUSE IN GORDON SQUARE,
A NINETEENTH-CENTURY AREA
OF LONDON MADE FAMOUS BY THE
BLOOMSBURY SET.
ITS IMPRESSIVE COLLECTION NUMBERS
OVER 1,400 CERAMICS FROM THE SONG,
YUAN, MING, AND QING DYNASTIES,
FROM THE TENTH TO THE EIGHTEENTH
CENTURIES.

*In the Palace alone are stored
  well-nigh a hundred dishes,
Yet bowls are as rare as stars
  in the morning.
What is there, indeed, for which
  a cause cannot be found?
Large bowls are difficult to
  preserve, small dishes easy.
In this I find a moral and
  a warning—
The greater the object, the greater
  the task of caring for it.*

THE Emperor Qianlong, over-come by the beauty and delicacy of an early twelfth-century Ru ware bowl—one of the rarest and most treasured types of Chinese ceramics—composed these lines in 1786 and had them inscribed inside this stoneware masterpiece. Those who have the good fortune to visit the Percival David Foundation of Chinese Art may contemplate this very bowl, notable for its finely crackled blue-gray glaze (described by archaeologists as "the color of ashes after burning"), its elegantly flared foot, and slender metal-bound rim, and study the inscribed characters of the Emperor's poem.

"Breathtaking" is the only word for the awesome ceramics and porcelains housed in this tranquil, light-filled oasis overlooking Gordon Square. Stoneware connoisseurs and scholars know the Percival David Foundation well, not just for its twelve outstanding pieces of Ru ware (more than any other collection outside China), but also for its exquisite celadons, its comprehensive collection of brilliant yellow, red, and turquoise

monochrome stoneware, and its outstanding translucent, hand-painted *famille verte* and *famille rose* porcelains, a number of which are aesthetically comparable to the finest Chinese scroll paintings. This collection also boasts an amazing variety of ceramic objects, including a lotus-shaped pipe, a flute decorated with gold, barrel-shaped garden stools with incised relief and enamel ornamentation, elaborate table screens once used for

decorative and inspirational purposes on scholars' desks, as well as burial pillows.

While the museum covers a period spanning the late tenth century to the eighteenth century, it also contains some important examples from the third and early fourth centuries, such as a group of Yue wares, notable for their greenish alkaline glaze—a remarkable feat, given the fragility of stoneware.

The most renowned pieces in the Foundation's collection are a pair of temple vases, the so-called "David Vases," made in 1351, considered the most important Chinese blue-and-white ceramics in the world. Not only is their painted decoration of the highest quality, they are also the *earliest* vases to bear dated inscriptions, at a time when most blue-and-white wares were made for export and, consequently, were not inscribed.

"The quality and the provenance of the pieces in the Percival David

Foundation collection have accorded it the reputation of being the most important collection of Chinese ceramics outside China," notes Stacey Pierson, the museum's assistant curator. "There are some people who say that it is the second best collection in the world, after the Palace Museum in Taiwan. It is an important collection because many of the objects have marks or inscriptions which enable us to precisely date them, and because a number of ceramics were formerly in the Imperial Collection," she adds.

That this incomparable collection, many of whose pieces were once housed in the Forbidden City, and which were reserved exclusively for use and viewing by the Imperial family, is in London at all, is a testimony to the perseverance of Sir Percival David (1892–1964), who assembled it and donated it to the University of London.

When David, a brilliant Sinologist and a pioneering scholar of Chinese art, learned in 1927, during a trip to China, that prospective buyers were endeavoring to acquire some of the Imperial Collection (which had been offered as collateral to the Yuin Yeh Bank by the Dowager Empress when she left the Forbidden City), he set about finding a way to buy it. So determined was he to secure these priceless ceramics, that he completely disregarded the fact that two other potential buyers had already been the target of death threats when they attempted to remove the objects from Beijing.

Not only was he able to overcome the many obstacles that arose during months of lengthy negotiation, he was also able to persuade the bank's board to accept his proposal. A selection of some forty pieces was made and the financial terms settled. Although the money was deposited accordingly, suddenly, without any

THESE REMARKABLE BLUE-AND-WHITE CERAMIC WARES LONG ASSOCIATED WITH CHINA,
MANY OF WHICH WERE MADE FOR EXPORT TO THE NEAR EAST AND LATER TO EUROPE,
DEMONSTRATE THE GREAT VARIETY OF DECORATIVE MOTIFS
RANGING FROM ELABORATE FLORAL DESIGNS TO DEPICTIONS OF DRAGONS AND
CHILDREN PLAYING. THE APOGEE OF BLUE-AND-WHITE CERAMICS
WAS THE XUANDE PERIOD (1426–1435).

warning, the bank did an about-face, arbitrarily repudiating the agreement and reneging on the transaction! As desperate as David was to obtain the treasures, he was flabbergasted by the bank's unscrupulous tactics. Fortunately, the friendly intervention of the bank's secretary put the negotiations back on track, and in the end, the transaction was completed to David's satisfaction.

The circumstances surrounding the collection's shipment overseas proved just as daunting. Consider Lady David's account in the catalogue *Percival David Foundation of Chinese Art:* "The chosen objects were divided by Sir Percival into three categories: the pieces of lesser quality were to be shipped first, to be followed by a second shipment, and the most precious pieces were to be shipped last. Now came the problem of their removal from Beijing. For this intricate operation, a close personal Japanese friend and, incidentally, an art dealer, was chosen, because he regularly made the round trip to his homeland.

"After the first shipment had cleared customs at Seoul, the dealer telegraphed Sir Percival, 'brother was in good health.' The same procedure was adopted for the second shipment. The transmission of the final and most precious cargo appeared in jeopardy when the eagerly awaited telegram reached Sir Percival saying

THESE STUNNING RED, YELLOW, AND GREEN STONEWARES
ARE FROM THE QING DYNASTY (1644–1911).
COPPER RED MONOCHROME STONEWARES WERE A PARTICULAR
CHALLENGE TO THE POTTER
SINCE THE FIRING TEMPERATURE HAD TO BE PRECISELY CONTROLLED
TO ACHIEVE THE BRILLIANT RED COLOR.

'brother ill and in hospital.' This disturbing news was quickly followed by the arrival at his hotel of the dealer's wife and six small children, the distraught lady demanding, 'What have you done with my husband?' Three days later, the [dealer] friend returned to relate the story of how he had celebrated with customs officials the successful conclusion of his mission, only to awake the next morning in jail! A guard was bribed to summon a local dealer friend to the prison, who was fortunately able to secure the Japanese dealer's release. From Japan, the treasures travelled across the United States, and are now displayed in all their glory at the Foundation."

Gazing at the objects in this collection, one cannot help but be struck by the level of sophistication among Chinese potters, at a time when European ceramic art was still in its infancy. Particularly remarkable is the stoneware from the Northern Song (960–1127) and the Southern Song (1127–1279) dynasties. Long before English creamware was invented, the coal-burning Ding kilns in the northern Hebei province were making stoneware in a warm ivory shade, with both incised and molded decoration. The largest proportion of these are open wares (bowls, dishes, and plates), although the Foundation is also very proud to display a superb example of a rare "teardrop"-shaped vase carved and incised with a decoration of peonies, a popular Ding ware motif.

The Song dynasty eventually abandoned Ding ware for celadon ware, whose glazes resembled jade in both color and texture. (In fact, the earliest celadons date to the Shang dynasty (1500–1050 B.C.) The term "celadon," used to describe green-glazed stoneware, is said to derive from the character Céladon in the pastoral romance *L'Astrée* by Honoré d'Urfé, published in 1610, whose gray-green costume bore a striking resemblance to the color of these Chinese ceramics. The museum's range of celadons alone is worth a visit: while some rely solely on the beauty of their glaze and the elegance of their form for their aesthetic appeal, others feature elaborate mold-ed decoration, or a crackle effect integral to the shape and design of the piece.

When the Percival David Foundation of Chinese Art opened in 1952, Sir Ralph Turner, Director of the School of Oriental and African Studies, remarked: "Surrounded by these superb examples of the art of a distant people and a distant age, to the collection and study of which that man devoted his life, our visitor will be well answered by the epitaph of Sir Christopher Wren in St. Paul's, London: '*Si monumentum requiris circumspice* (If you seek his monument look around.').'" Thanks to the passion and dedication of one man, such a "monument" exists, celebrating one of the world's oldest arts and offering visitors hours of pleasurable discovery and enriching contemplation.

THIS EXQUISITELY SIMPLE RU WARE BOWL FROM THE NORTHERN SONG DYNASTY (EARLY TWELFTH CENTURY) CONTAINS AN INSCRIBED EIGHTEENTH-CENTURY POETIC DESCRIPTION COMPOSED BY THE EMPEROR QIANLONG. (COURTESY PERCIVAL DAVID FOUNDATION OF CHINESE ART.)

Design Museum

Shad Thames
London SE1 2YD
Tel: 0171–403–6933

**Open Monday through Friday
11:30 A.M. to 6:00 P.M.;
Saturday and Sunday
Noon to 6:00 P.M.**

**Underground: Take the District
or Circle Line to Tower Hill,
then walk across Tower Bridge
to Butler's Wharf, and follow
signs leading to the Design
Museum.**

Coffee bar on premises.

WITHOUT the widespread consumption of tea and coffee in eighteenth-century England, the tea kettle might never have been invented. Before, water was boiled in a pot suspended from a hook over an open fire. It would take nothing less than England's coal industry, which supplied the iron, steam, and electrical industries, to generate the first affordable, mass-produced cast-iron, copper, and brass kettles and make them a fixture in British homes.

Although the first electric kettles were invented early in this century, it was some time before they were widely adopted. Not only was electric power expensive and limited in availability (only six percent of English homes were wired for electricity in

THE DESIGN MUSEUM, THE WORLD'S FIRST MUSEUM OF INDUSTRIAL DESIGN,
OFFERS A SWEEPING VIEW OF LONDON AND THE THAMES.
OPEN SINCE JULY 1989, IT HOUSES THREE GALLERIES AND A STUDY CENTER;
OBJECTS ON DISPLAY INCLUDE CARS, FURNITURE,
DOMESTIC APPLIANCES, CAMERAS, PENS, AND CERAMICS.

1918), but it was distrusted by a great many people. Consequently, early electric kettles derived their shape from the conventional saucepan and the traditional teapot to inspire consumer confidence.

Still, as late as 1935, only half of British homes were wired for electricity and the electric kettle's market penetration was less than ten percent. It would take the success of the Spitfire aluminum airplane in World War II to make electric tea kettles popular. Impressed by the lightness and improved heat conduction of aluminum, ideal qualities for cooking implements, manufacturers introduced aluminum kettles that began to sell rather well.

This fascinating history of the ubiquitous electric kettle is illustrated through objects and recounted through informative signboards at the sleekly modern and pristine Design Museum overlooking the Thames, the world's first institution devoted to the evolution of industrial design in the twentieth century. Opened in 1989, the museum is the inspiration of Sir Terence Conran of Habitat and Conran Shop fame.

"Our intent is to demonstrate the social, cultural, and economic reasons for design," explains Leslie Butworth, the museum's educational director. "We are not a taste palace nor an arbiter of taste. Our aim is to show the extraordinary history behind

THIS DISPLAY ILLUSTRATES THE DEVELOPMENT OF ELECTRIC
TEA KETTLES IN THE TWENTIETH CENTURY, SHOWING KETTLES
IN ALL SHAPES, SIZES, AND MATERIALS.

everyday objects we take for granted, and to show why they are interesting, provocative, and successful from a commercial standpoint."

The objects on display in the permanent collection (the museum regularly holds temporary exhibitions) range from tableware, televisions, and radios to desklamps, typewriters, and office furniture.

Even the most mundane objects have an interesting story behind them. For instance, the relaxation of dining rituals and the development of materials technology have had a substantial impact on tableware. With the growing desire for convenience and practicality, new materials such as stainless steel, heat-resistant glass, and synthetic plastics have engendered designs that are multifunctional, more durable, easier to clean, and in some cases, disposable.

Sometimes, the styling has emphasized function: one example is David Mellor's design for cutlery for the elderly and disabled, which takes into consideration an impairment of the hands. The handles are large for easy gripping, and each utensil combines two functions of either cutting and grasping, or scooping and grasping.

Some design innovations, such as dishes made of melamine (which were first developed in the 1930s), weren't introduced into the home until after World War II. Melamine not only was heat, dye, and water-resistant, but it also allowed designers to depart from traditional ceramic shapes; for instance, a handle became an extension of a cup, instead of being attached to it separately.

The museum also demonstrates how, in recent decades, industrial design has taken into consideration

TELEVISION STYLING BECAME A KEY FEATURE OF SETS MADE IN THE SEVENTIES, AND MANY
MODELS WERE INFLUENCED BY CONTEMPORARY FURNITURE DESIGN; SOME DESIGNERS
EVEN WENT SO FAR AS TO USE UNUSUAL MATERIALS AND SHAPES, SUCH AS THIS WOODCHIP
FRAMED TELEVISION, TITLED "JIM NATURE" BY FRENCH DESIGNER PHILIPPE STARCK.

the "human factor" by inventing a science known as "ergonomics." Derived from the Greek words *ergon* and *nomos,* which together mean "the laws of work," this discipline addresses the relationship between people and the tools and equipment they use, be they cars, typewriters, writing instruments, or computer terminals and keyboards. Among the critical factors taken into consideration are the size and strength of people's bodies, safety concerns, the layout and legibility of controls or keyboards—even the use of color to identify the particular functions of a product.

A perfect example of an ergonomically designed product is the *Bobby Trolley,* designed by Joe Colombo and manufactured by Bieffeplast in Italy: a light, mobile, and flexible storage unit on wheels made of injection-molded plastic, so easy to use that it is even recommended for the disabled.

One can see that prior to ergonomics, office furniture was often designed to restrict rather than enhance human activities. This motivation is evident in the awkward, heavy metal desk, known as the "Minister's Desk" manufactured in pre-war France by Strafor, and in the industrial drawing of a "Modern Efficiency Desk"—little more than a desk with three shallow drawers—which apparently was intended to prevent office workers from stowing away papers and overlooking important documents.

Knowing that pocket-size solar calculators are as thin and as light as matchbooks, it's hard to conceive that less than a century ago, businesses relied on the forbidding, cumbersome "comptometer," a primitive calculating machine, first developed in the 1880s by Dorr Eugene Felt. The comptometer followed on the heels of the manual typewriter, and used keys instead of levers. The first one could only be used for adding and was made out of a cigar box! The museum's American model made by Felt & Tarrant (c. 1914) used the British currency system and incorporated an epicyclic gear mechanism allowing for more complicated calculations. (This type of machine was used until the 1950s, when the electronic calculator began coming into general use.)

One of the most fascinating exhibits is the Baird Televisor, the world's first television receiver. Developed by John Logie Baird in 1924, the museum's 1929 model (which resembles an old-fashioned liquor cabinet), received a low-definition thirty-line signal which was picked up as a tiny, orange flickering image that could be stabilized using two control knobs. The story of Baird's invention is a tribute to human ingenuity: his first television receiver was built from household odds and ends, including a porcelain sink and a biscuit tin, and was held together with darning needles, pieces of string, and sealing wax! (While Baird was the first to demonstrate television as a working concept, similar research was being carried out in continental Europe and in the United States.)

On November 10, 1936, the world's first daily, domestic television broadcasting service was transmitted by the British Broadcasting Corporation from London's Alexandra Palace. A pre-war television set cost as much as a family four-door sedan, and transmission lasted for just two hours a day, six days a week. It's not surprising that only an estimated four hundred sets were in use during that launch year.

THIS WOODEN MODEL OF THE AUTOMAXIMA WAS CREATED IN 1989 BY TETRA ASSOCIATES, GREAT BRITAIN, FROM LE CORBUSIER'S UNREALIZED 1928 WORKING DRAWINGS. USING AERODYNAMIC PRINCIPLES, AND OFFERING MAXIMUM VISIBILITY, LE CORBUSIER'S CAR WAS INTENDED TO BE MODERATELY PRICED, CATERING TO THE NEEDS AND COMFORT OF THE DRIVER.

THIS COMPTOMETER OR PRIMITIVE CALCULATOR, ADJUSTED TO THE BRITISH CURRENCY
SYSTEM, WAS MADE BY FELT & TARRANT IN THE UNITED STATES (C. 1914).
DEVELOPED IN THE 1880S BY DORR EUGENE FELT, THE FIRST MACHINE WAS MADE
OUT OF A CIGAR BOX AND COULD BE USED ONLY FOR ADDING.

Early televisions were designed as pieces of furniture in their own right, and their styling showed a strong Art Deco influence. However, by the late 1930s, television sets shrank in size and became less expensive. The outbreak of World War II brought the BBC television service to a sudden halt half-way through a Mickey Mouse cartoon. The shutdown was essential—if the BBC had continued to broadcast, it would have provided an ideal beacon for enemy aircraft. After the war, television technology improved so significantly that by 1953 an estimated 2.5 million sets were in use in Great Britain. Queen Elizabeth's Coronation that year made television a household word (an additional 500,000 sets were purchased to watch the televised event, which was seen by 20 million people worldwide).

Part of the thrill in visiting this elegant and informative museum is seeing that everyday objects one has come to take for granted—be they the telephone, the television, the automobile, the home computer, or the camera—were usually developed through trial and error and have not always been readily accepted by consumers. Very often, industrial designs have become indispensable necessities only through the clever and imaginative application of engineering, marketing, and advertising techniques. Learning more about their often surprising chronology, one cannot help but marvel at the talent and energy that have made their realization possible.

Dickens House Museum

**48 Doughty Street
London WC1N 2LF
Tel: 0171–405–2127**

**Open Monday through Saturday
10:00 A.M. to 5:00 P.M.**

**Underground: Take the Piccadilly
Line to Russell Square,
then walk to Doughty Street.
Bus: 19, 38, 45, 55**

DICKENS CELEBRATED THE
FIRST ANNIVERSARY OF HIS MARRIAGE
ON SUNDAY, APRIL 2, 1837,
PROBABLY THE SAME WEEKEND
HE MOVED WITH HIS SMALL FAMILY INTO
48 DOUGHTY STREET,
NOW THE DICKENS HOUSE MUSEUM.
HIS FAVORITE FLOWERS, RED GERANIUMS,
ARE PLANTED IN THE WINDOW BOXES.

WHEN the twenty-five-year-old English novelist Charles Dickens (1812–1870) moved to 48 Doughty Street, a three-story terraced house in Bloomsbury, in April 1837, he was celebrating both his first year of marriage to Catherine Hogarth and the enormous success of the *Pickwick Papers.* Located on an elegant private road attended by porters in mulberry-colored livery and gold-lace trimmed hats whose job was to keep unwanted callers away, this Regency home was a notable improvement over the author's cramped quarters at Furnival's Inn. Dickens moved here with his small family, which included his wife Catherine, their first-born son Charles, who was nearly three months old, and Dickens's younger brother Fred.

In the two years (April 1837 to December 1839) he lived at Doughty Street, the multifaceted, prolific young author completed the last six monthly installments of the *Pickwick Papers,* as well as wrote and published *Oliver Twist* and *Nicholas Nickleby.* He also penned *Sketches of Young Gentlemen,* edited the *Memoirs of Joseph Grimaldi* (the famous English clown) under his pen name "Boz," and found time to write *The Lamplighter,* a farce for the English actor William Macready (which was neither performed nor published during his lifetime). It was also here that he began work on *Barnaby Rudge,* an historical novel based on the anti-Popery riots of 1780.

Yet, less than a month after this auspicious move, tragedy struck the happy, prosperous household. After an outing to the theater, Catherine's

THE DRAWING ROOM HAS BEEN RECONSTRUCTED AS IT LIKELY WAS IN THE AUTUMN OF 1839, SHORTLY AFTER DICKENS HAD COMPLETED *NICHOLAS NICKLEBY*. AMONG THE ITEMS THE NOVELIST OWNED ARE THE ARMCHAIR UPHOLSTERED IN PLUM-COLORED HIDE, THE CANE-BOTTOM CHAIRS, THE ÉTAGÈRE FOR MUSIC SCORES, AND THE LARGE RECTANGULAR TABLE.

sister Mary Hogarth collapsed, and died of a heart seizure in Dickens's arms the following morning. The novelist, who had doted on Mary's charm and liveliness, was so overcome by her death that he was unable to work. The publication of the *Pickwick Papers* was temporarily halted, as was that of *Oliver Twist*, which, as editor of *Bentley's Miscellany*, Dickens was beginning to serialize. Only after a rest in Hampstead was Dickens able to resume writing. Still, he kept Mary alive in his thoughts, drawing upon her personality and appearance for the character of Rose Maylie in *Oliver Twist* and later for Little Nell in *The Old Curiosity Shop*.

Under normal circumstances, Dickens was not only exceptionally productive, but he could also easily accommodate interruptions from guests and members of his household while in the midst of writing. His brother-in-law Henry Burnett recalled how during one evening at Doughty Street, Dickens joined the conversation of his guests while working on his monthly installment of *Oliver Twist:* "While he was pleasantly discoursing he employed himself in carrying to a corner of the room a little table, at which he seated himself and recommenced his writing. We, at his bidding, went on talking 'our little nothings'; he, every now and then (the feather of his pen still moving rapidly from side to side), put in a cheerful interlude."

While 48 Doughty Street (now the

IN THE FORMER DINING ROOM, WHERE DICKENS ENTERTAINED
THE ILLUSTRATOR GEORGE CRUIKSHANK, THE POET AND ESSAYIST LEIGH HUNT,
AND THE PAINTER DANIEL MACLISE, IS A GRANDFATHER CLOCK FROM
THE OFFICE OF BATH COACH PROPRIETOR MOSES PICKWICK.
(IT WAS AFTER HIM THAT DICKENS NAMED HIS HERO OF THE *PICKWICK PAPERS*.)

Dickens House Museum, which first opened in June 1925) has undergone significant changes since its rising young author lived here, it remains an invaluable aide-mémoire for both enthusiasts and scholars. It is here that one can find the quill pen Dickens used when writing his last, unfinished novel, *The Mystery of Edwin Drood,* the reading glass he worked with from 1834 until his death in 1870, the tooled morocco leather flip-top desk upon which he wrote until the end of his life, and the very chair he used at the weekly newspaper *All The Year Round,* which he edited until two weeks before his death.

A tour of the museum's ten rooms provides an opportunity to better understand how Dickens researched and wrote his books, how he developed, directed, and performed plays for both his friends and family, how he organized the readings of his works, and how his extraordinary energy enabled him to live several different lives, all in the span of less than sixty years. This restless genius not only wrote incessantly, but also found time to launch four magazines and a daily newspaper, to run a home for reclaimed prostitutes, to lobby for a much-needed change in copyright laws, to pioneer mesmerism and early forms of psychotherapy, to travel widely in America and Europe, and to maintain a hectic social schedule, often in the company of such friends as Jane and Thomas Carlyle, Henry Wadsworth Longfellow, and William Makepeace Thackeray.

"I hope visitors who come to this museum go away knowing more about Dickens," says the curator, Dr. David Parker, who bears an uncanny resemblance to an 1886 portrait of the novelist by William Power Frith, now hanging in the study. "I also hope they gain a sense of his milieu and his home, and the importance of both."

Most of the museum's rooms are used to exhibit an abundance of carefully documented portraits, photographs, letters, and manuscripts, as well as personal memorabilia, much of it displayed inside large glass cases. Only the fully furnished drawing room on the second floor (completed by the Heritage of London Trust in 1983) provides a glimpse of how Dickens decorated and entertained. A microscopic examination of paint scrapings revealed that the novelist chose lilac for the woodwork, a good match for the lilac trellis-patterned wallpaper that is appropriate for the period, although not of his choosing. Late Regency styles prevail in the furnishings—many of which once belonged to Dickens, including an armchair upholstered in plum-colored hide, cane-bottom chairs with soft leather cushions, a small round tripod-footed table, an étagère for musical scores, and a large rectangular table.

The drawing room's brilliant red silk curtains trimmed with black fringe are a fitting theatrical touch in keeping with the man who regularly entertained his friends with dramatic renditions of his novels. A striking gilt-frame mirror hangs above the marble fireplace mantel and brass fenders, which were also chosen by Dickens. Mirrors had a special significance for this novelist, who used them to make faces and act out the different parts and dialogue of

THIS OLD TRADESMAN'S EMBLEM OF THE GOLDBEATER'S RAISED ARM WIELDING A HAMMER, WHICH DICKENS USED TO PASS DAILY IN SOHO, WAS LATER WRITTEN OF IN *A TALE OF TWO CITIES*.

his characters, before committing their words to paper.

The museum's wealth of memorabilia reveals to what lengths Dickens —a journalist by training—took his inspiration from the sights and sounds of London, as well as from mementos that had great meaning to him. For instance, the delicate turquoise stone-set engagement ring that Dickens gave his wife Catherine Hogarth in 1836, was evoked by him as the ring that David Copperfield gave to Dora, "a pretty little toy, with its blue stones." On the landing of the handsome Regency staircase leading to the second floor is the original of the "Little Wooden Midshipman," memorably described in *Dombey and Son*.

Two of the rooms in the museum —the novelist's bedroom and dressing room—have been named the "Suzannet Rooms," because they contain an outstanding collection of Dickensiana, assembled and donated by Comte Alain de Suzannet (1882–

1950). One display case in the bedroom contains a superb collection of original drawings for illustrations in Dickens's books, by such artists as Robert Seymour, H.K. Browne ("Phiz"), John Leech, and Clarkson Stanfield. Seymour's sketch of *The Dying Clown* for the second install-ment of the *Pickwick Papers* seems all the more poignant when one learns that it was the last thing he worked on before his suicide in 1836. Interestingly enough, the novelist

William Makepeace Thackeray applied directly to Dickens to replace Seymour; however, Dickens ultimately chose to work with Browne instead.

While Victorian England would have preferred that Dickens remain a happily married paterfamilias with nine children, the reality proved sadly different. In 1858, he shocked both his family and society by separating from his wife, Catherine, after many years of marriage and providing her with another establishment. (He kept

A CHELSEA WARE MONKEY INSPIRED DICKENS'S
FERTILE IMAGINATION AS HE WROTE AT HIS DESK IN GAD'S HILL
(WHERE HE RESIDED AFTER LEAVING DOUGHTY STREET).
THE MONOGRAMMED SILVER NAIL CLIPPER, THE MAGNIFYING GLASS,
THE DELICATE COIN PURSE, EVEN HIS QUILL PEN,
ARE AMONG THE EXTENSIVE DICKENSIANA ON DISPLAY.

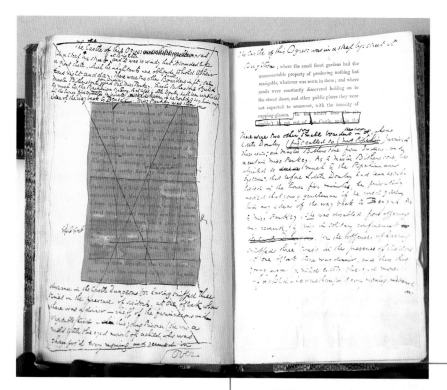

ONE OF DICKENS'S PROMPT BOOKS
THAT HE USED FOR HIS DRAMATIC READINGS
IS REPLETE WITH HIS CUTS AND
STAGE DIRECTIONS.

all the children with him with the exception of his eldest son, Charley, who was instructed to live with his mother.) The museum displays an affecting letter to the noted English philanthropist Angela Burdett-Coutts, in which he wrote about his separation: "Nothing on Earth—no, not even you—no consideration human or Divine, can move me from the resolution I have taken. . . . "

Thanks to the museum's careful scholarship and abundant displays, visitors are able to discover the multifaceted nature of Dickens—showing that while he could be fascinating, gregarious, and generous, he was also intensely human, easily slighted, and often melancholy.

While it seems a pity that one can no longer share a chop and a chat

with Dickens at Doughty Street, as he often invited his friends in to do, the Dickens House Museum gives visitors a chance to become pleasurably acquainted with the man who once lived here and who was destined to become one of the world's best-read and most admired authors.

Dulwich Picture Gallery

College Road
London SE21 7AD
Tel: 0181-693-5254

Open Tuesday through Friday
10:00 A.M. to 5:00 P.M.;
Saturday 11:00 A.M. to 5:00 P.M.;
Sunday 2:00 P.M. to 5:00 P.M.

Underground: Take the Victoria
Line to Brixton, then take the P4
bus to the Dulwich Picture Gallery.
Bus: 3 from Oxford Circus,
Piccadilly Circus, Trafalgar Square
and Westminster to West Dulwich
Station, then walk about ten
minutes to the Gallery.
By car: The Gallery is 500 meters
from the South Circular Road,
A205, and is easily accessible
from Central London on the A23.
(There is ample free parking.)

THE DULWICH PICTURE GALLERY,
THE FIRST PURPOSE-BUILT GALLERY
IN GREAT BRITAIN,
CHALLENGED CONVENTION WITH
ITS PLAIN BRICK FAÇADE, FLAT
PILASTERS, AND LACK OF DECORATION
OR AN ARCHITECTURAL ORDER.

SOMETIMES one nation's misfortune is another's stroke of good luck. A perfect case in point is the Dulwich Picture Gallery. Despite its verdant suburban locale and modest size, this museum boasts an outstanding collection of Old Masters that any national museum would be proud to own.

It is here that one will find Rembrandt van Rijn's affecting *Portrait of A Young Man* (possibly the artist's son Titus), about which the English critic William Hazlitt wrote: "Nothing can be richer than the coloring, more forcible and masterly than the handling and more consistent and individualized than the character of the face." Adjacent to it is an example of his earlier finely detailed style in the *Portrait of Jacob III de Gheyn,* about which De Gheyn's brother penned this couplet:

> *This is Rembrandt's hand and*
> *Gheyn's face*
> *Marvel, reader, this is but is*
> *not Gheyn.*

It is only here that one can admire, as the English painter John Constable once did, Antoine Watteau's *Les Plaisirs du Bal,* showing a playful, yet wistful, gathering of French courtiers, which prompted him to write: "The picture seemed painted in honey; so mellow, so tender, so soft, so delicious . . . be satisfied if you touch but the hem of his garment, for this inscrutable and exquisite thing would vulgarize even Rubens and Paul Veronese."

These seventeenth- and eighteenth-century masterpieces—a fraction of the riches on display— were initially brought together by the discerning art collector and dealer, Noel Desenfans (1745–1807) for the King of Poland, Stanislas Augustus, who had asked him to assemble a collection of paintings for the national gallery he wished to establish in Warsaw.

Unfortunately, in 1795 the Kingdom of Poland ceased to exist after it was overrun and its land divided among Austria, Prussia, and Russia. Stanislas was forced to move to St. Petersburg, leaving Desenfans with the pictures. Failing in his efforts to sell the collection either to the British or the Russian governments, Desenfans opted to retain the nucleus of the collection and build upon it, with the ultimate aim of bequeathing it to Great Britain upon his death. Put simply, Poland's loss has proven to be England's gain.

Persuaded that his country needed a national gallery where young artists could study the works of the Old Masters, in 1799 Desenfans published *A Plan* for setting up such a gallery at no expense to England. However, because the British government was embroiled in the Napoleonic Wars, it ignored his proposal. Undeterred by this reaction, Desenfans decided to create his own public gallery containing his collection and, in this endeavor, continued to purchase paintings, with the help of his friend, the Polish court painter Sir Francis Bourgeois. Upon his death, his entire collection was left to Bourgeois, with the proviso that he should select an institution that would preserve and exhibit it.

After much deliberation, Bourgeois decided to bequeath the paintings to Dulwich College, which already possessed a modest gallery displaying works given by its founder Edward Alleyn (1566–1626), the famous actor-manager, and by William Cartwright (1606–1686), a fellow

actor turned bookseller. Oddly enough, only 80 of the 239 pictures that were in Cartwright's legacy reached Dulwich: most of his estate was taken by his servants who claimed —when taken to court—that they had not been paid for eleven years!

The Alleyn and Cartwright paintings, some of which are on display, are important because they provide rare depictions of leading actors of the seventeenth century. Among them is the only known portrait of Richard Burbage (1567–1619), Shakespeare's partner and fellow actor, who created the roles of Richard III and Hamlet.

In 1811, Bourgeois commissioned his close friend the English architect Sir John Soane (already well known for such buildings as the Bank of England) to construct a freestanding picture gallery that would also contain a mausoleum and almshouses for poor women. Intrigued by the assignment, and the unorthodox building that it would require, Soane waived his fee, viewing the project as his tribute to Desenfans and Bourgeois.

After substantial delays caused by the College's inability to meet the original cost estimate (only resolved by Mrs. Desenfans's offer of financial assistance), the first stage of the Gallery was completed in 1814, at a cost of 8,778 pounds. The original building consisted of five galleries, three square and two oblong, with almshouses on either side of a centrally placed mausoleum. It opened its doors to the public in 1817, thus besting the National Gallery by seven years as the first public art gallery in Great Britain. Work continued on the Gallery after it had opened; when it was completed, the total cost of the building had risen to 14,222 pounds.

In the late nineteenth century, the almshouses were converted into galleries, and additional exhibition

THE MUSEUM'S INTERIOR
GALLERIES ARE
WELL PROPORTIONED AND
INGENIOUSLY LIT
BY A SERIES OF SKYLIGHTS,
WHICH AVOIDS THE
USE OF SIDE WINDOWS.

space was added at the beginning of this century to accommodate later bequests of eighteenth-century English painting (including works by Thomas Gainsborough, Thomas Lawrence, and William Hogarth) given by the talented English composer Thomas Linley (1733–1795) and Charles Fairfax Murray, an eccentric and reclusive collector who trained as a young painter under Sir Edward Burne-Jones (1833–1898), and who was closely associated with the Pre-Raphaelites.

Strolling through the finely proportioned interior galleries, one is struck by the way they are ingeniously lit by a series of skylights providing sufficient light to avoid glare and the use of side windows. While the building's lack of exterior decoration and plain brick façade (which were unusual for the time), were widely criticized during Soane's lifetime, contemporary architects such as Frank Gehry and Robert Venturi, who designed the National Gallery's Sainsbury Wing with Denise Scott-Brown, praise Soane's design and acknowledge their debt to his pioneering work.

The mausoleum, the only one of its kind in a public British museum, is in two parts: the first is an antechamber with a sunken floor and Greek Doric peristyle capped with a shallow saucer dome, to give the effect of a temple; the second, a lantern-lit sepulchre filled with funeral urns and sarcophagi of Portland stone, containing the bodies of Bourgeois and Mr. and Mrs. Desenfans. Dramatically lit by amber glass skylights, the mausoleum has an appropriately grandiose and awesome atmosphere, further enhanced by the closed Greek doors that convey the message that no one returns from the House of the Dead.

Although the mausoleum was extensively damaged during the Second World War by a German V-1 "doodlebug," which landed across the street, Soane's plans proved so detailed that it was possible to restore both rooms to their original state.

In his 1835 *Memoirs,* Soane wrote of his achievement: "We have only to fancy the Gallery brilliantly lit for the exhibition of this unrivalled assemblage of pictorial art—whilst a dull religious light shews the Mausoleum in the full pride of funereal grandeur, displaying its sarcophagi enriched with the mortal remains of departed worth, and calling back so powerfully the recollections of past times, that we almost believe we are conversing with our departed friends who now sleep in their silent tombs!"

Visitors to the Dulwich Picture Gallery can certainly be grateful to these unorthodox patrons for having the aesthetic discernment and generosity that now makes it possible to contemplate some of the finest works in Western European painting in a setting that was remarkable in their time and remains so to this day.

IN *LES PLAISIRS DU BAL* BY ANTOINE WATTEAU (1684–1721)
THE FIGURES ARE SET ON A STAGE-LIKE TERRACE
AND DRESSED IN RUBENSIAN COSTUME;
ALTHOUGH THE SCENE DEPICTED IS ONE OF FROLIC,
THE PAINTING'S OVERALL MOOD SEEMS DREAMY AND WISTFUL.
(REPRODUCED BY PERMISSION OF
THE TRUSTEES OF DULWICH PICTURE GALLERY.)

Duxford Airfield
Duxford
Cambridge CB2 4QR
Tel: 01223–835000

Open every day except December 24, 25, 26; Summer (March 16– October 26) from 10:00 A.M. to 6:00 P.M.; Winter from 10:00 A.M. to 4:00 P.M.

Disabled Access.

- By train: Take British Rail from Liverpool Street Station or Kings Cross Station to Cambridge, then take a local bus to the museum.
- By bus: There is a daily coach service from Victoria Coach Station London to Cambridge that includes a stop at the museum.
- By car: Take the M25 motorway from London to Duxford (approximately one hour travel time).

Self-service restaurant on premises.

DURING World War II, the Duxford Operations Room was a central focus of perilous and top-secret activity. Even now, more than half a century after the war's end, a palpable tension still hangs over the room, as one listens to the sounds of sirens, interrupted by voices speaking in a coded language. On the wall is a scoreboard indicating the air squadron numbers and their positions. An enormous map shows the area they are protecting east of England. On the wall are signs that read "Don't Help the Enemy!," "Careless Talk Costs Lives," and "Careless Talk May Give Away Vital Aircrafts."

Today, this historic room is empty, and visitors from all over the world can speak as they wish. Almost sixty years ago, in June 1940, this same locale was a vital nerve center during the Battle of Britain, the intensive air fighting that opposed Hitler's attempt to dominate the skies over England as a prelude to invasion.

It was from this very airfield, east of Cambridge, that the Royal Air Force fighter command played a vital role in repulsing Germany's Luftwaffe, including such heroes as Flying Officer Douglas Bader, who had lost both his legs in an air crash several years earlier, but who did not allow his artificial limbs to deter him from serving as a courageous pilot and becoming an exceptional leader of men. (While undertaking ground duties at Duxford in 1933, Bader, who had been discharged from the RAF as permanently unfit, badgered the RAF until he was allowed to rejoin.)

THIS P-47 THUNDERBOLT,
CHRISTENED "BIG BEAUTIFUL DOLL,"
CARRIES THE MARKINGS OF
THE UNITED STATES 78TH FIGHTER GROUP,
BASED AT DUXFORD
BETWEEN 1943 AND 1945.

By the end of August 1940, the Commander-in-Chief of 12 Group, Air Vice-Marshall Trafford Leigh-Mallory, had ordered the Hurricanes of the 242 Squadron, now commanded by Bader, down from Coltishall, to join the 19 and 310 Squadrons on daily standby at Duxford. So impressed was he by the performance of these latter two squadrons that Leigh-Mallory authorized Bader to lead all three as a Wing. By this time, the Luftwaffe had turned their attention to London. On September 9th, the Duxford squadrons announced they had destroyed twenty of the enemy, losing only four Hurricanes and two pilots.

Because of this crucial victory, two more squadrons were added to the Wing, which soon became known as Bader's "Big Wing." This Wing, formally known as 12 Group Wing, was ready for action by September 15, 1940, which later became known as "Battle of Britain Day." On this historic day, they took to the air twice against Luftwaffe attacks, claiming by evening to have destroyed forty-two enemy aircraft.

Duxford, which became part of Great Britain's Imperial War Museum in 1977, also has a special meaning for Americans, since in April 1943, the airfield was handed over to the United States 8th Airforce, the largest of the Army Air Forces at the time, with 200,000 men serving at its peak. Duxford now became Base 357 and the headquarters of the 78th Fighter Group, which flew P-47 Thunderbolts and acted as a fighter escort to the large American bomber raids in occupied Europe, and Germany itself. On D-Day, June 6, 1944, the long-awaited beginning of the Allied invasion of Normandy, every available 78th Fighter Group Thunderbolt was giving air cover to the Allied invasion fleet as it crossed the Channel. By the end of the war, the 78th was credited with the destruction of 697 enemy aircraft either in the air or on the ground.

Today, Duxford—which saw its last operational RAF flight in July 1961— is dedicated to the presentation, conservation, and restoration of this century's military and civilian aircraft. The breadth and scope of its collections are so extensive that it is regarded as the largest and most important aviation museum in Europe. The only flying that is done from its airfield (little changed from the days when it belonged to the Royal Air Force) is recreational in nature, and a source of enjoyment for visitors.

Its collection of historic airworthy aircraft ranges from bombers such as the Boeing B-17 Flying Fortress "Sally-B" (star of the film *Memphis Belle*), Spitfires and Hurricanes, to examples of the Bearcat, Hellcat, and Corsair. Even the Luftwaffe is represented by two German World War II fighters, a Spanish-built Messerschmidt Bf109J and the Bf109G owned by the Ministry of Defense. This is the only German combat aircraft still flying anywhere in the world that actually saw wartime action.

All these aircraft are maintained in mint flying condition, and are put through their paces in demonstration

VISITORS TO DUXFORD'S AIRPLANE HANGARS CAN SEE VINTAGE WAR PLANES, SUCH AS THOSE SHOWN HERE, BEING RESTORED BY VOLUNTEERS.

BY THE TIME THIS SHACKLETON XF-708 (FOREGROUND) REACHED DUXFORD IN AUGUST 1972, IT HAD FLOWN OVER 6,500 HOURS AND HAD MADE ALMOST 2,500 LANDINGS.

have been handsomely restored, and have great appeal to military history buffs, the museum has added a sobering touch of reality by exhibiting the kind of devastating destruction they could inflict. "By showing the kind of damage that could have been done, we give the exhibit a human scale," notes Francis Crosby, Duxford's deputy head of marketing and public relations. "Our aim is to place each weapon in context. We don't glorify war here, but we try to tell people how it was. Our goal is to give people the facts."

Duxford's close ties with America are reflected not just in its past, but also in its outstanding agglomeration of American military aircraft from World War II and after—a collection viewed as the finest and most comprehensive outside the United States. That is why Duxford was felt to be a fitting site for the new American Air Museum in Britain, designed by the eminent British architect Norman Foster. This museum is not only a tribute to the American airmen of World War II, recording the critical role of United States air power in the conflict, but also documents American military aviation history in Korea, Vietnam, NATO, and the Gulf War. Among the eighteen planes on display, some of which are suspended from the building rafters, is the U-2 spy plane (which was shot down over Soviet airspace in the 1950s), and a replica of the Grumman Avenger, a World War II torpedo plane that President George Bush flew as the youngest naval aviator in the Pacific Theater. It is hard to miss, with the name of his wife "Barbara" on the nose—a decorative touch that Bush was glad to approve.

Unlike the practice at many other museums, at Duxford the conservation and restoration of exhibits is accomplished in full view of visitors,

VISITORS CAN CLIMB
INSIDE THE
CONCORDE JET
PARKED PERMANENTLY
AT DUXFORD
AND EXAMINE THE
COCKPIT'S INTRICATE
INSTRUMENTS
AT CLOSE RANGE.

flights during the summer. Duxford's airfield is ideally situated for staging air shows, and each year several special events are held here, such as the Classic Fighter Air Show and the Duxford September Air Show.

One of the newest attractions at Duxford is the Land Warfare Hall, which houses the museum's impressive collection of tanks, trucks, and artillery dating from World War I to the Gulf War. Although the weapons

DUXFORD'S IMPRESSIVE DISPLAY OF ARTILLERY
DATING FROM WORLD WAR I
PROVIDES A GRIM REMINDER OF
TRENCH WARFARE, WHICH DEPENDED HEAVILY
ON THE BRITISH HOWITZER (SHOWN HERE)
AND THE FIELD GUN.

thus offering a fascinating glimpse into the interior of an aircraft. Wherever possible, Duxford's aircraft and vehicles are restored to full working condition, often with the aid of volunteer ex-aircraft engineers and pilots, as well as aviation buffs.

Duxford, with its historic military and civilian aircraft from all over the world, is a unique museum that demonstrates how particular weapons of war have been used to secure the peace. By paying homage to a wide array of flying machines, and to the people who built them, maintained them, and flew them, this historic locale provides a source of stimulating yet thoughtful reflection on aviation's past, present, and future.

Museum of Eton Life

Eton College
Windsor
Berkshire SL4 6DB
Tel: 01753–671177

Open every day during the school term from 2:00 P.M. to 4:30 P.M.; open during holidays from 10:30 A.M. to 4:30 P.M. Groups must make an advance appointment to visit the museum. (Hours are governed by the school terms, school events, and services held within the College Chapel.)

- **By train: Take the Waterloo Line from Waterloo Station to Windsor & Eton Riverside. Walk across Windsor Bridge and follow the signs to Eton College and the Museum of Eton Life.**
- **By car: Take the M4 from London, take Exit 6 to Windsor, park in Windsor, then walk across Windsor Bridge to Eton College and the Museum of Eton Life.**

In 1440, when he was all of eighteen, young King Henry VI founded "The King's College of Our Lady of Eton" beside Windsor, intending that it should provide accommodation and education for seventy poor scholars free of charge. The school was to be part of a large establishment that included a community of secular priests, ten of whom were Fellows or priests, a pilgrimage church, and an almshouse for the poor. To fulfill his ambitious program, Henry lavished on Eton a substantial income from land, as well as a huge collection of holy relics (among which were supposed to be fragments from the Holy Cross and the Crown of Thorns).

By 1443, the world's oldest continuous classroom (Lower School) and dormitory (Long Chamber) had been completed; by 1450, College Hall, where priests, headmaster, and scholars ate together, was in use. Unfortunately, the Lancastrian Henry VI never lived to see his enterprise completed, for in 1461 he was assassinated in the Tower of London and supplanted by his rival Yorkist claimant, Edward IV. Overnight, Parliament annulled all grants of Lancastrian lands, including those of Eton, while the religious ornaments and relics were transferred to St. George's Chapel at Windsor. Tradition has it that Edward's mistress, Jane Shore (whose Confessor was Provost at Eton College), was influential in persuading the King to maintain the College, albeit on a smaller scale.

It was out of this complex and tumultuous history that Eton,

England's largest and most famous public school was born, a history that now spans five and a half centuries, and which is now charmingly illustrated and documented at the Museum of Eton Life. Located in the handsomely restored undercroft, which was once used as a cellar for the Provost and Fellows' wine and the King's Scholars' beer (which was brewed at Eton until 1875), this museum reveals the unique culture and rituals that have given the school its mystique and reputation.

While Eton is generally regarded as the epitome of the proper English gentleman's "public school," it is interesting to learn that some of its most famous graduates changed the course of world history in a variety of ways. These include the Duke of Wellington, victor at the Battle of Waterloo and later Prime Minister, Prime Minister Sir Harold Macmillan, the scientist Robert Boyle, "the father of modern chemistry," the poets Percy Bysshe Shelley, A.C. Swinburne, and Thomas Gray, and the novelists Henry Fielding, Aldous Huxley, George Orwell, and Ian Fleming. Two of Eton's graduates, Thomas Lynch and Thomas Nelson, signed the American Declaration of Independence.

The museum's collection of drawings and memorabilia reveal that the school's strictly regimented and spartan existence, which prevailed from the mid-sixteenth through the mid-nineteenth century, was hardly

THIS PHOTO OF THE FIVE GOSLING BROTHERS (MAX, MA, MI, MIN, QUINT)
TAKEN IN 1888 DEMONSTRATES TYPICAL NINETEENTH-CENTURY ETONIAN ATTIRE.
THE THREE YOUNGEST BROTHERS WEAR "BUM FREEZERS"
(SHORT JACKETS WORN BY BOYS UNDER FIVE FEET FOUR INCHES IN HEIGHT).
TOP HATS WERE ABANDONED IN 1940; "BUM FREEZERS" IN 1964.

for the fainthearted. Its seventy scholars, who slept two to three to a bed in the Long Chamber (the large dormitory in use for four hundred years), were locked in each evening and left with practically no supervision until the next day.

Awakened at five in the morning, they chanted prayers while they dressed, and were at work in the Lower School by six. All teaching was conducted in Latin, the language of the Church, the law, and business. The boys ate two daily meals except for Fridays, which was a fast day. Lessons finished at eight in the evening, at which time the students were sent to bed, after saying their prayers. At all times during the day, the boys were closely supervised by "praeposters" or monitors appointed by the headmaster, whose job was to note absentees, enforce the speaking of Latin, and check for uncleanliness. Older boys lorded it over younger

ones, and it was here that the tradition of "fagging" began, with younger pupils being obliged to do menial jobs for older ones, including cooking food and cleaning boots. (It was only in the 1970s that this time-honored tradition ended.)

One exhibit is devoted to Dr. Keate, Eton's longest serving and most notorious headmaster, (1809–34), a formidable orator, scholar and disciplinarian, and also the last to teach all the senior boys (who could number as many as 200 in a class). To maintain classroom order, Keate often resorted to public beatings of his pupils; after one disturbance he flogged eighty boys in an evening, after another, a hundred! The museum illustrates his formidable reign with a display that includes his Napoleonic tricorne hat, flogging birches, and a "swishing block" (the latter was used for public whippings of insubordinate students).

Even if Eton's academic reputation under Keate remained high, living and teaching conditions were so poor that by 1841 half the places remained unfilled. Not only had the food become monotonous and unappetizing, breakfast and tea were no longer even provided. A complete lack of supervision in the Long Chamber made bullying rampant, and many of the younger boys lived in terror of the older ones. Far-reaching reforms were undertaken by Keate's successor, Francis Hodgson, who revised the curriculum to include mathematics, science, and modern languages, recruited more assistant masters, and built new schoolrooms in order to reduce the size of the classes.

A video describing daily life at Eton today demonstrates the relationship between continuity and change at the College. There are still seventy scholars, fifteen of whom are selected each year in June on the basis of a competitive examination. They live together in "College," which consists of the New Buildings added in 1846 and the original Long Chamber, now divided into separate study-bedrooms. The number of Oppidans (regular students who live in twenty-four separate boarding houses, each run by a housemaster with an average of fifty boys per house) has risen to twelve hundred. Each house also has a resident matron, known as the Dame, who is respectfully addressed by the boys as "Ma'am."

Flogging was abolished in the mid-Sixties, and today's punishments vary from writing out Latin lines to

THIS SENIOR BOY'S ROOM (C. 1900) SHOWS THE TABLE SET FOR "MESSING TEA."
TYPICAL OF A BOY'S ROOM EVEN TODAY ARE THE "BURRY" (DESK), THE ARMCHAIR,
AND THE WALLS COVERED WITH PICTURES AND A BOATER,
REMINDERS OF ETONIAN TRADITIONS.

THE BRONZE STATUE BY FRANCIS BIRD IN THE MIDDLE OF ETON'S SCHOOL YARD
WAS ERECTED IN 1719 BY PROVOST HENRY GODOLPHIN.
THE STATUE'S LATIN INSCRIPTION READS: "HENRY GODOLPHIN PROVOST OF THIS COLLEGE
PUT UP THIS STATUE TO THE ABIDING MEMORY OF
THE MOST PIOUS PRINCE HENRY VI, KING OF ENGLAND AND FRANCE, LORD OF IRELAND,
AND THE MOST MUNIFICENT FOUNDER OF ETON."

weeding the housemaster's garden. While students still wear the traditional black morning tail suit with a white shirt, and some senior boys still sport the famous Etonian winged-collar and white bow tie—the attire of a nineteenth-century gentleman—top hats were abandoned in 1940 and "bum freezers" (short jackets worn by boys under five feet four inches tall) were dropped in 1964.

The museum's exhibits show that sport has played a central role in the life of the average Etonian. While the College is well-known for boating (the Eton College Boat Club is the largest boat club in the world in terms of both members and boats), it has also proven very inventive in creating new games: the Wall Game, the Field Game, and Fives, all of which have a long history. The Wall Game, which is illustrated by a number of period photos and illustrations, is noted for its muddy conditions, the rarity of any goals being scored, and the obscurity of its rules, even though it enjoys a very high prestige. The museum also pays photographic homage to Lord Burghley, Eton's most famous athlete, who won the 400-meter hurdles at the 1928 Olympics (he is represented as "Lord Lindsay" in the 1980 film *Chariots of Fire*).

While there has always been a close association between the College and the monarchy, no sovereign showed more interest nor became more Etonian at heart than George III, who proved to be the school's second great royal patron. The College deeply respected and loved the King, whose birthday, the Fourth of June, was made an annual holiday. To this day, it is celebrated with

THIS SILVER GILT MODEL OF ETON COLLEGE CHAPEL
WAS PRESENTED TO THE SCHOOL
BY KING WILLIAM IV.

"Speeches," cricket, and a procession of boats on the river. Among the museum's more colorful displays is a Fourth of June procession boat in full regalia.

Perhaps the final stanza in "The Eton Boating Song," written by the headmaster William Cory for the Fourth of June 1863, best conveys the special affection that Etonians hold for their school, and which is so amply demonstrated in this novel museum:

> *Twenty years hence this weather*
> *May tempt us from office stools:*
> *We may be slow on the feather,*
> *And seem to the boys old fools:*
> *But we'll still swing together,*
> *And swear by the best of schools.*

Freud Museum

**20 Maresfield Gardens
London NW3 5SX
Tel: 0171–435–2002**

**Open Wednesday through Sunday
Noon to 5:00 P.M.**

**Underground: Take the Jubilee
Line to Finchley Road, then
follow the signs indicating the
Freud Museum up a steep
alleyway to Maresfield Gardens.**

SIGMUND FREUD
LIVED IN THIS HOUSE WITH
HIS FAMILY FROM SEPTEMBER 1938
UNTIL HIS DEATH
AT THE AGE OF EIGHTY-THREE
IN SEPTEMBER 1939;
HIS DAUGHTER ANNA LIVED
HERE UNTIL HER DEATH IN 1982.
FOLLOWING A PERIOD OF
RENOVATION,
THE FREUD MUSEUM OPENED IN
JULY 1986.

THOSE familiar with the life
and work of Sigmund Freud (1856–
1939) the founder of psychoanalysis,
tend to associate him with Vienna and
his residence at 19 Berggasse Strasse,
where he lived and practiced for
almost half a century. It may come as
a surprise to discover that it is in a
quiet residential street in North
London that one will find the famed
original Persian carpet-covered couch
upon which patients reclined comfortably, while Freud, out of sight,
listened attentively to their "free
association" (saying anything that
came to mind without consciously
sifting or selecting information), the
method upon which psychoanalysis
was built.

A refugee from the Nazis, Freud
moved to this house on September
27, 1938 (after a brief stay at 39
Elsworthy Road), and remained here
until his death at eighty-three on
September 23, 1939, barely three
weeks after the start of World War II.
He had left Vienna with great
reluctance, despite the fact that his
works and those of fellow psychoana-
lysts were publicly burned in 1933
and that other members of the
predominantly Jewish psychoanalytical
community had already emigrated.
Only after Austria had been annexed
by Germany, his house draped with
the banner of a swastika, and his own
family subjected to Nazi harassment
(Anna, the youngest of the psychoanalyst's six children, was arrested on
March 22, 1938, and held for a day
by the Gestapo for questioning),
did Freud finally consent to leave.

Freud's escape to London, accompanied by his spouse, Martha, his

FREUD'S FAVORITE ANTIQUITIES STAND LIKE SENTINELS
WATCHING OVER THE PSYCHOANALYST'S DESK;
PRIDE OF PLACE IS GIVEN TO A FOUR-INCH-HIGH ROMAN COPY
OF A FIFTH-CENTURY B.C. ATHENA,
THE ONE PIECE FREUD ASKED MARIE BONAPARTE TO SMUGGLE
OUT OF AUSTRIA IN CASE HIS WHOLE COLLECTION
WAS CONFISCATED BY THE AUTHORITIES.

daughter Anna, his son Ernst, his sister-in-law Minna Bernays, and his housekeeper Paula Fichtl, was made possible through the intervention of William C. Bullitt, the first American ambassador to the Soviet Union, and a former patient of the psychoanalyst. (Ernest Jones, Freud's biographer, and Princess Marie Bonaparte, herself a psychoanalyst and former patient, also provided vital assistance in obtaining the family's emigration papers.) This mandatory flight proved costly: like other Jews in a similar plight, the Freud family was forced to pay a "refugee tax," which amounted to one-quarter of their estimated assets. Freud was granted his wish to "die in freedom" in England, the country whose literature and politics he most admired.

Knowing that Freud was grievously ill with cancer of the palate (he suffered from this disease for the last sixteen years of his life), his family and friends extended themselves to make him feel comfortable in his new home. His son Ernst, an architect, designed the loggia overlooking the rear garden and added an elevator that enabled the increasingly frail Freud to move more easily between his study and library on the ground floor and his living quarters on the second floor. Despite his illness, Freud continued to work: *Moses and Monotheism* was completed in this house, and his final work, *Outline of*

THIS DRAWING OF SIGMUND FREUD BY FERDINAND SCHMUTZER
DREW MUCH PRAISE FROM THE SITTER, WHO WROTE TO THE ARTIST:
"IT GIVES ME GREAT PLEASURE AND I SHOULD REALLY
THANK YOU FOR THE TROUBLE YOU HAVE TAKEN
IN REPRODUCING MY UGLY FACE,
AND I REPEAT MY ASSURANCE THAT ONLY NOW DO I FEEL
MYSELF PRESERVED FOR POSTERITY."

Psychoanalysis, was written here as well. Moreover, for as long as he was able, Freud maintained his practice and received a number of patients for analysis.

After Freud died, his daughter Anna, herself a psychoanalyst, remained at 20 Maresfield Gardens, where she lived and practiced, specializing in the field of child psychology. In 1986, the Freud family home was transformed into the Freud Museum, as Anna had wished.

What makes this museum unique is that under a single roof one can learn about the life and work of the father of psychoanalysis and that of

his daughter (a pioneer in the study of child development), while at the same time admiring one of the world's most outstanding private collections of Egyptian, Greek, Roman, and Chinese antiquities, amassed lovingly and assiduously by Freud for the greater part of his life, and which he had been able to save and take with him when he left Vienna in 1938.

On the ground floor is Freud's study and library, preserved as they were when the psychoanalyst was alive. The study, which had been carefully reconstructed to resemble the one that Freud left behind in Vienna, is saturated with antiquities, most of

THE ORIGINAL ANALYTIC COUCH
THAT WAS BROUGHT FROM BERGGASSE 19 IN VIENNA,
UPON WHICH PATIENTS WOULD RECLINE
COMFORTABLY, WHILE FREUD—
SEATED OUT OF SIGHT IN A GREEN VELVET
TUB ARMCHAIR—LISTENED TO THEIR
"FREE ASSOCIATION."

THE MAIN THRUST OF FREUD'S COLLECTION—
NON-FRAGMENTARY EGYPTIAN, GREEK, AND ROMAN FIGURINES—
IS ILLUSTRATED IN THIS CROWDED VITRINE OF ANTIQUITIES.
DISCUSSING THE IMPORTANCE OF HIS COLLECTION,
FREUD WROTE TO NOVELIST STEFAN ZWEIG:
"I HAVE MADE MANY SACRIFICES FOR MY COLLECTION OF
GREEK, ROMAN AND EGYPTIAN ANTIQUITIES,
AND ACTUALLY HAVE READ MORE ARCHAEOLOGY THAN PSYCHOLOGY."

which were acquired from dealers in Vienna. His passion for collecting ancient artifacts was apparently only second to his addiction to cigars. "I have made many sacrifices for my collection of Greek, Roman and Egyptian antiquities," he once wrote to the Austrian novelist Stefan Zweig, adding, "and actually have read more archaeology than psychology."

While this declaration may seem affable hyperbole, a visit to the Freud Museum reveals how much the psychoanalyst's extensive assemblage of antiquities (there are over 2,000 in the collection) influenced and even dominated his life and work. They also had a lasting impact on his analysands, judging by the recollections of one of the most famous, known as "the Wolf Man": "Here were all kinds of statuettes and other unusual objects, which even the layman recognized as archaeological finds from ancient Egypt. Here and there on the walls were stone plaques representing various scenes of long-vanished epochs. . . . Everything here contributed to one's feeling of leaving the haste of the modern world behind, of being sheltered from one's daily cares. Freud himself explained his love for archaeology in that the psychoanalyst, like the archaeologist in his excavations, must uncover layer after layer of the patient's psyche, before coming to the deepest, most valuable treasures."

While circumstances prevented Freud from bringing all of his books from Vienna, nonetheless the library at Maresfield Gardens does contain those works he elected to bring with him, and demonstrates the wide range of subjects that absorbed his scholarly mind: art, literature, archaeology, philosophy, and history, as well as psychology, psychoanalysis, and medicine. The bookshelf behind Freud's desk contains some of the authors he loved most, including Shakespeare, Goethe, Dostoyevsky, Flaubert, and Anatole France—writers who, he acknowledged, had gained insights into the unconscious that psychoanalysis later tried to explain systematically.

While the museum is largely a tribute to the life, work, and collections of Sigmund Freud, the Anna Freud Room reveals varying aspects of her work and personality, as well as memorabilia associated with her life and interests. This room contains her own analytic couch and a loom that she once used. Anna was a keen weaver and knitting enthusiast; this latter activity is one she practiced during her analysis sessions with patients. As early as 1910 Anna had begun reading her father's work, but her serious involvement with psychoanalysis began in 1918, when her father began psycho-analyzing her—something that was not unusual for the times. In 1920 they both attended the International Psychoanalytical Congress at The Hague.

After 1923, when Freud was stricken with cancer, he became increasingly dependent on his daughter's care and nursing. His illness was the reason why a "Secret Committee" was formed to protect psychoanalysis against attacks. Anna was a member of this committee and, like the others, was given a ring as a token of trust. After her father's death, she converted one of the rings into a brooch, now on display in the museum; the Roman intaglio bears the figure of Jupiter enthroned, crowned by Victory with Minerva in attendance, an apt metaphor for the relationship between Anna and her father.

Following the outbreak of World War II, Anna set up the Hampstead War Nursery, which provided foster care for over eighty children. After the war, a group of orphans from the Theresienstadt concentration camp were entrusted to the care of Anna Freud's colleagues at the Bulldogs Bank home, a situation that inspired her to write about children's ability to find substitute affections among their peers, in *An Experiment in Group Upbringing*. Together with psychoanalyst Dorothy Burlingame (who lived at Maresfield Gardens until her death in 1979), Anna also published studies of children under stress: *Young Children in War-Time* and *Infants Without Families*. While the Freud Museum demonstrates how Anna Freud's work was a continuation of her father's, it also reveals her own diligent and far-reaching search for useful social applications for psychoanalysis, above all in treating and learning from children. "I don't think I'd be a good subject for biography," she once commented laughingly. "You would say all there is to say in a few sentences—she spent her life with children!"

Today, 20 Maresfield Gardens has come to represent the symbolic home of psychoanalysis. Like the ancient statuary of sphinxes that Freud so liked to collect, this is a museum replete with compelling riddles, be they about the man who lived and worked here, his daughter, or the myriad artifacts that meant so much to them both. These very riddles, which represent the complexity of the human mind, hold the same compelling fascination today as they once did for Sigmund Freud.

ANNA FREUD'S ROOM CONTAINS HER ANALYTIC COUCH
AND A LOOM THAT SHE KEPT IN HER BEDROOM.
SHE WAS A KEEN WEAVER AND A KNITTING ENTHUSIAST,
THE LATTER ACTIVITY BEING ONE THAT
SHE PRACTICED DURING ANALYSES OF HER PATIENTS.

FREUD'S SPECTACLES
AND EYEGLASS CASE
LIE ON ONE OF
HIS SPRAWLING DIARY
ENTRIES.
HE KEPT A JOURNAL
UNTIL THE
END OF HIS LIFE.

Museum of Garden History

Lambeth Palace Road
London SE1 7LB
Tel: 0171-261-1891

Open Monday through Friday
10:30 A.M. to 4:00 P.M.;
Sunday 10:30 A.M. to 5:00 P.M.
March to November.

Underground: Take the Bakerloo
Line to Lambeth North Station.
Bus: 3, C10, 77, 344, 507

Coffee bar on premises.

THE site of Great Britain's only museum devoted to the history of gardening has undergone a striking transformation since its director, Rosemary Nicholson, first came upon the Church of St. Mary-at-Lambeth over twenty years ago. "For nine hundred years St. Mary's was the parish church of Lambeth. Yet in 1972, the church ceased to be used for worship and was closed," she recalls. "As time went on, it became increasingly derelict. Vandals destroyed much of the glass in the windows and the churchyard became a rubbish heap and the haunt of vagrants. Gradually, the building fell into decay and by 1976 plans had been made for its demolition," she adds.

Fortunately, thanks to Nicholson's determined and herculean efforts, the Church of St. Mary-at-Lambeth was spared this dismal fate. The church lies next to Lambeth Palace—home of the Archbishop of Canterbury—on the banks of the Thames, directly opposite the Houses of Parliament. The first of five successive churches on the same site was built in 1062 by the Countess Goda, sister of Edward the Confessor. Six Archbishops of Canterbury are buried on its grounds.

Reopened in 1983, the Victorian church has been transformed into the Museum of Garden History—a shrine to England's gardens and notable gardeners, welcoming experts as well as amateurs from all over the world. Today, the edifice's honey-colored Kentish ragstone has been scrubbed clean, its stained-glass windows restored, and its ancient churchyard has been beautifully landscaped with a seventeenth-century knot garden,

THE FORMER CHURCH OF ST. MARY-AT-LAMBETH
(NOW HOME TO THE MUSEUM OF GARDEN HISTORY)
LIES NEXT DOOR TO LAMBETH PALACE
ON THE BANKS OF THE THAMES,
DIRECTLY OPPOSITE THE HOUSES OF PARLIAMENT.

which offers a fragrant and colorful assortment of flowers, plants, and shrubbery (some of which are cited in the Old Testament).

Although the five-hundred-year-old church tower no longer rings with the peal of bells, it still beckons visitors to discover the history of the two John Tradescants, who were among England's most eminent gardeners and plant-hunters (their carved stone sarcophagus lies in the churchyard, next to that of Captain Bligh, of *Mutiny on the Bounty* fame).

The story of the Tradescants—a story filled with courage, scholarship, and exploration—is vividly recounted at the Museum of Garden History. It begins in the reign of Elizabeth I, during which the elder John Tradescant (c. 1570–1638) was born. With the nation at peace, it was a

THE TRADESCANT GARDEN AT ST. MARY-AT-LAMBETH
FEATURES A KNOT GARDEN AND THE TOMBS OF THE TRADESCANTS AND CAPTAIN BLIGH,
OF *MUTINY ON THE BOUNTY* FAME.

period of great expansion, discoveries, and increasing wealth. Young adventurers were exploring the world, bringing back flowers, trees, and shrubs to stock the gardens of the English nobility's palatial country estates. One mansion was particularly notable—Hatfield House in Hertfordshire, the property of Robert Cecil (later the first Earl of Salisbury and principal secretary to Queen Elizabeth I), who appointed Tradescant as his gardener. Traveling widely throughout Europe,

Tradescant brought back large quantities of trees and plants, including cherry, apple, quince, medlar, mulberry, and pear trees, as well as red, white, and black currants, and flowers such as roses, fritillaries, and gillyflowers—all of which are grown in the museum's garden. Among the important specimens he procured on a diplomatic trip to Russia was the larch tree, which provided England with timber, as well as bark for tanning and turpentine.

Tradescant also began a unique

THESE FREESTANDING PANELS DISPLAY
A RARE GROUPING OF VICTORIAN
GARDENING TOOLS AND GLASS CLOCHES.

collection of one-of-a-kind curiosities, including a Russian abacus, "Powhatan's Mantle" (the oldest extant garment from North America), a stuffed dodo, fossils, insects, weapons, medals—even a stuffed tiger's head. This fascinating compilation was displayed in Tradescant's Lambeth home "The Ark," reputedly the world's first museum open to the public. One visitor who went there reported: "A man might in one day behold . . . more curiosities than he should see if he spent his life in travel." A 1656 edition of the *Musaeum Tradescantium,* which provides an inventory of the Tradescants' museum, and was once the property of the English gardener and diarist John Evelyn, is the Museum of Garden History's most precious possession.

John Tradescant the Younger (1608–1662), who took over his father's position as royal gardener, inherited his passion for plant and curiosity hunting, traveling three times to North America, a voyage that required three months each way. While it is impossible to determine the exact number of plants that the intrepid Tradescant introduced to the British Isles, it is safe to say that England owes him the tulip tree, the swamp cypress, the yucca plant, the columbine, and the plane tree from North America, new species of roses, bulbs, and all sorts of fruit trees from Europe, as well as the apricot tree from North Africa.

Before Tradescant the Younger died in 1662, he became friendly with his next-door neighbor Elias Ashmole, and supposedly while "distempered" (inebriated) willed him the treasures of The Ark by deed of gift. (While he later tried to have the deed annulled, the English courts ruled that it was valid.)

Ashmole then succeeded in persuading Oxford University to build a museum (first opened in 1683) to house this prized "collection of rarities." All the credit for the collection thus went to Ashmole, in whose honor the Ashmolean Museum was named (now the Museum of the History of Science), while the energy and enterprise of the Tradescants went largely unacknowledged. It wasn't until 1978 that the museum opened a room to house what remained of the Tradescants' "rarities." While denied the honor of having the world's first public museum named after them, the Tradescants have nonetheless given their name to a family of perennials, the *Tradescantia* (spiderwort), and to the Tradescant Trust, which administers the Museum of Garden History.

With its rare seventeenth-century "watering pots," eighteenth-century seed sowers, and nineteenth-century clear glass cucumber straightener, Victorian gardeners' smocks, Edwardian garden furniture, and three-penny pamphlet entitled *Cloches versus Hitler* by Charles Wyse-Gardner, which provided tips on the growing of food during World War II, the museum features the same sort of eclecticism that must have characterized The Ark.

Perhaps the most unusual item on display is the "Vegetable Lamb of Tartary," a fern species whose unusual shape was remarked upon in various travelers' accounts as far back as the eleventh century. This rare fungus, of which only a half-dozen are said to be in existence, was dubbed the "vegetable lamb" because its roots resembled a baby lamb.

While the Victorians had a taste for the exotic, they also brought about a revolution in gardening through the same technology that fueled the Industrial Revolution. Among the era's innovations on prominent display are the lawn mower, the secateur (a type of pruning shears invented by the French), as well as brass syringes and sprayers, which were used for pest control and the elimination of weeds.

The museum displays an early version of the lawn mower, which was invented by Edwin Beard Budding in 1830. An engineer from Gloucestershire, who worked in the woolen mills, Budding had the inspiration for this invention after examining the way machines cut the nap of woven materials. "The invention of the lawn mower made it possible for middle-class families to have lawns—something that was previously reserved for the grand houses of the wealthy, where dozens of men once were employed to cut the grass with scythes," notes Rose Lea, the museum's curator.

One innovation, whose formula died with its creator, is "coade stone," invented by Eleanor Coade in the eighteenth century. This composite

GERTRUDE JEKYLL'S MINIATURE ENAMEL FLOWERS
WERE USED TO DECORATE
QUEEN MARY'S DOLLHOUSE AT WINDSOR CASTLE.

stone, which has proven to be far more resistant to weathering and pollution than ordinary stone, was used for building and statuary, including the exquisite statue of the *Charity Boy,* carved around 1785 and displayed in the museum.

Besides paying tribute to the Tradescants, Captain Bligh (who imported breadfruit from the Pacific Islands to the West Indies so that it could be grown as slaves' food), and Lancelot "Capability" Brown, England's first landscape consultant, the museum has dedicated a section to the celebrated garden designer Gertrude Jekyll, who was deeply interested in the color relationships between different blooms.

A comprehensive exhibit documenting the entire history of gardening since its inception is slated for the future. "While we may have the biggest collection of gardening tools in the United Kingdom, this museum is still in its infancy," observes Lea. "We hope visitors who come here will appreciate that gardening and garden design is very much an art form. We also want to make it possible for them to share in the many delights and intriguing aspects of garden history."

Geffrye Museum

**Kingsland Road
London E2 8EA
Tel: 0171–739–9893**

**Open Tuesday through Saturday
10:00 A.M. to 5:00 P.M.;
Sundays and Bank Holiday
Mondays 2:00 P.M. to 5:00 P.M.**

**Underground: Take the Circle Line
to Liverpool Street, then Bus 22A,
22B, or 149 from Bishopsgate,
or take the Northern Line to
Old Street, then Bus 243 to the
museum.
Bus: 22A, 22B, 67, 149, 243
Train: Dalston Kingsland or
Liverpool Street.**

**Coffee bar: open 10:15 A.M. to
4:30 P.M.**

THE GEFFRYE ALMSHOUSES
WERE BUILT IN 1715
BY THE WORSHIPFUL COMPANY OF
IRONMONGERS,
WITH FUNDS FOR THAT PURPOSE
LEFT BY SIR ROBERT GEFFRYE,
THE FORMER LORD MAYOR OF LONDON.

WHEN Shakespeare lived in London, most of the city's population resided in houses built of timber, lit by rushlights dipped in tallow, and relied on the nearest street pump or conduit for their supply of water. It would take the Great Fire of 1666, which destroyed two-thirds of the city, to move the authorities to ban the building of wooden houses and mandate that all dwellings be built of brick.

By the eighteenth century, houses of the well-to-do were laid out as residential estates, which were terraced along wide streets and around squares. A piped-in water supply to the kitchen permitted washing up with basins, and even the occasional bath. Many rooms had fireplaces with small iron grates for burning coal instead of wood and were lit with candles, either in candlesticks, wall sconces, or candelabra.

While such living arrangements have become a thing of the past, visitors to the Geffrye Museum in Shoreditch, London, can rediscover them in beautifully appointed rooms that present a panorama of four hundred years of British home furnishings and interior design. The visit begins with the seventeenth century, noted for its oak furniture and paneling, then proceeds to elegant Neoclassical interiors of the Georgian period, followed by the middle-class opulence of the Victorians, the privations of the Blitz, and the lively utilitarian decor of postwar Modernism.

As the only museum in the United Kingdom to show a specialist collection of English furniture and decorative arts in a chronological series, the Geffrye Museum permits visitors to survey the changes in taste and society that have influenced home decorating and the domestic arts. The museum takes its name from Sir Robert Geffrye (1613–1704), twice Master of the Worshipful Company of Ironmongers, who rose to prominence during the Restoration, when he was knighted by Charles II and appointed Lord Mayor of London. A wealthy man, he left part of the fortune he made in trade with Africa and India to the Ironmongers' Company "to purchase a convenient piece of ground, in or near the City of London whereon to erect and build an Almshouse for so many poor

THIS AWARD-WINNING HERB GARDEN,
FORMERLY AN ABANDONED, OVERGROWN SITE NEXT TO THE MUSEUM,
PROVIDES A HAVEN OF BEAUTY AND BOTANICAL INTEREST
IN THE EAST END, AN AREA KNOWN IN THE SEVENTEENTH AND EIGHTEENTH CENTURIES
FOR ITS INNOVATIVE NURSERIES.

THIS LATE GEORGIAN DRAWING ROOM,
USED FOR FORMAL ENTERTAINING,
SUCH AS LADIES' TEA PARTIES
AND MUSICAL RECITALS,
EXEMPLIFIES THE PREFERENCE FOR
INLAID FURNITURE DURING THIS PERIOD.
IT WAS LARGELY INSPIRED BY
GEORGE HEPPLEWHITE,
WHOSE MOST CHARACTERISTIC DESIGN
WAS THE SHIELD-BACK CHAIR.

people as the monies . . . may extend or amount unto." The austere yet handsome buildings, which comprise fourteen houses and a chapel, were constructed in 1715 and served as a retirement home for pensioners and widows for almost 200 years.

In 1908, after the Ironmongers Company decided to build alms-houses in a less populated part of the city, the buildings and grounds were acquired by the London County Council, which considered demolishing two wings to increase the size of the gardens. Fortunately, as the result of a petition signed by members of the Arts and Crafts Movement, urging that the almshouses be converted into a museum for the "Education of Craftsmen," the buildings were saved

THIS TUDOR CHRISTMAS CELEBRATION
INCLUDES "HEDGEHOG" SWEETMEATS
MADE FROM MARZIPAN AND "EGGS"
MADE OF SWEET DOUGH;
THE ARRANGEMENT OF HOLLY, IVY, AND
MISTLETOE WITH APPLES
AND ORANGES HANGING BENEATH,
WAS KNOWN AS "THE KISSING BOUGH."

from demolition, and the Geffrye Museum was opened in 1914. Thanks to informative, illustrated wall panels, the period rooms take on an even greater significance, enabling visitors to appreciate more fully how people once lived and entertained.

During the course of the seventeenth century, English interiors reflected a growing desire for comfort and convenience. Heavy oak furniture and rough woolen textiles were gradually replaced by more delicate furnishings, influenced by imports from the Continent and the Far East. As the influence of the Italian Renaissance spread through Europe, classical motifs such as strapwork and grotesques were mixed with the earlier Gothic geometric and floral patterns in both Elizabethan and Jacobean furnishings.

Although there was little inspired decorating during the English Civil War and the Glorious Revolution, after the restoration of Charles II in 1660 Baroque decoration became the fashion, with an emphasis on ornamental scrolls, crowns and shells, and an increased usage of imported tapestries and textiles. Following the accession of William of Orange in 1688, the Dutch style was exported to England, as evidenced by the museum's Queen Anne period room, which is furnished with high-backed ebonized beech chairs, a mirror with a marquetry frame made of walnut veneer inlaid with boxwood, ebony, and ivory, and blue-and-white English-made Delftware.

An early Georgian period room, representing the parlor or "closet" in the town house of a wealthy London merchant, presumably was used by the family and close friends for informal social gatherings, such as playing music or drinking tea. London's rapid development and prosperous trade with her colonies

in America, the West Indies, and the Far East are reflected in the room's imported goods and materials, such as the card table made of Cuban mahogany and the fine Chinese porcelain. The high quality of English craftsmanship in furniture in this period was partly inspired by the many skilled Protestant Huguenots who sought refuge in England from religious persecution in France.

With the advent of the Industrial Revolution in the nineteenth century, mass-produced, inexpensive, and durable "yellow stock" brick became the standard building material for houses in London. Wallpaper was hung in the parlor, dining room, and bedrooms, while tiles tended to be used in halls, stairways, and kitchens. Floors were covered with rugs and carpets. Gaslights became common in the parlor, dining room, and hall, and were supplemented by paraffin table lamps. The kitchen range heated the water, which generally had to be carried up several flights of stairs by servants to the bedrooms above. Only rarely did water get piped under pressure to the bath and washbasins upstairs.

The favored reception room was the front parlor, where important guests were received, and where the furnishings reflected the taste and wealth of the family. Bold color schemes, achieved through new chemical dyes, were often featured in the carpets and furnishings. In an era when highly ornate decoration was a sign of prosperity and elevated social status, homes tended to be filled with large quantities of furniture, pictures, and knick-knacks, all of which are amply represented in the museum's cluttered mid-Victorian morning room.

In contrast to this excess, the late nineteenth century's Arts and Crafts movement drew its inspiration from

THIS REGENCY DRAWING ROOM
REVELS IN DECORATION,
AS EVIDENCED BY THE BLUE-AND-WHITE
DESIGN IN THE WALLPAPER,
THE DECORATIVE WHITE MARBLE FIREPLACE
MANTEL, THE ZEBRA-WOOD BRASS-INLAID
CARD TABLE, AND THE HIGHLY ORNATE
SILVER TEA-SET.

the simplicity of Medieval and Cottage architecture and furniture. Led by William Morris, the movement sought to encourage fine craftsmanship and a respect for the honest use of good quality materials, as evidenced by the handsome oak furniture designed by C.F.A. Voysey in the museum's Edwardian period room. Because of the intensive hand labor involved, such furniture was reserved only for the wealthy, although the design precepts of Morris and his followers were to have a profound influence on architecture and interior design in this century.

While the Geffrye Museum doesn't expose the terrible housing conditions of the British working class, it does underscore the impact of World War II, when only people whose homes had been destroyed and young

THIS SMALL STUDY FROM
AN 1880S VICTORIAN VILLA,
DECORATED IN THE AESTHETIC STYLE,
EXHIBITS A STRONG
FAR EASTERN INFLUENCE—MOST NOTABLY
JAPANESE—AS SHOWN
IN THE ELABORATE WALLPAPER,
EBONIZED FURNITURE,
AND BLUE-AND-WHITE CERAMICS.

couples just starting out were allowed new furniture under the "Utility Scheme," which ran from 1941 to 1951. Because of a shortage of materials, both the design and manufacture of furniture were subject to controls. Only government-approved products stamped with the CC41 logo could be made and sold. The wartime room with its drawn black-out curtains, and its stirring recording of *"There'll Be Bluebirds Over The White Cliffs of Dover,"* provides an unexpected touch of poignancy.

The tour concludes with a zany and colorful 1950s-style living room, decorated in bold colors and abstract patterns, a reaction against postwar austerity. The influence of contemporary art on British textile design can

THIS FIFTIES-STYLE LIVING ROOM,
DECKED OUT FOR A HOLIDAY PARTY,
IS BASED UPON ILLUSTRATIONS
IN MAGAZINES AND HOME DECORATING MANUALS.
IT FEATURES PLAIN, NON-SUITE FURNITURE
IN PALE WOOD POPULARIZED BY THE G-PLAN,
AND TEXTILE DESIGNS
IN BOLD COLORS AND ABSTRACT PATTERNS
INSPIRED BY CONTEMPORARY ART.

be seen in the "Rug Splash" pattern in the Tomkinson area rug, reminiscent of the splatter paintings of Jackson Pollock.

The Geffrye Museum's curatorial staff has assembled an impressive and adaptable display of British home furnishings and interior design, so that the decor of the various rooms can reflect successive seasons.

Moreover, it is possible for the visitor to personally assess the sturdiness and comfort of the fine reproductions of period chairs. This enchanting museum is an elegant treat, providing a glorious tribute to many admirable aspects of British interior design, while inviting one and all to step into the past, where they will soon find themselves feeling entirely at home.

Dr. Johnson's House

**17 Gough Square
London EC4
Tel: 0171–353–3745**

**Open Monday through Saturday
11:00 A.M. to 5:30 P.M.
October to April 11:00 A.M. to
5:00 P.M.**

**Underground: Take the Central
Line to Chancery Lane or the
District Line to Blackfriars.
Bus: 11, 15, 23, 26, or 75. Get off
at the first stop after Fetter Lane,
then walk through either Johnson's
Court, Bolt Court, Hind Court,
or Wine Office Court, all of which
lead to Gough Square.**

DR. JOHNSON'S ONLY EXTANT HOUSE
IN LONDON, 17 GOUGH SQUARE,
MIRACULOUSLY SURVIVED THE
ONSLAUGHT OF A FLAMING OIL DRUM
FROM A NEARBY PRINTER'S INK FACTORY,
WHICH HAD BEEN HURLED ONTO
ITS ROOF DURING A BOMBING RAID
OVER LONDON IN 1940.

SITUATED within a labyrinth of walkways and passages, in the heart of London's Fleet Street area, lies a handsome and inviting Queen Anne brick house that can best be described as a memorial to the English language, for it was here that Dr. Samuel Johnson (1709–1784) compiled the first comprehensive English dictionary.

Of the many houses in London in which Johnson lived (his eminent biographer James Boswell lists seventeen), 17 Gough Square, built around 1700, is the only one that is extant: an isolated, four-story private house dwarfed by a complex of surrounding office buildings. When Johnson lived on Gough Square (he spelled it G-o-f-f), the rent was thirty pounds a year (about 3,000 pounds or $4,500 in present-day purchasing power). After he left, the house was occupied with declining status until 1911, when it was acquired, restored, and opened as a museum by Cecil Harmsworth, later Lord Harmsworth, a Liberal MP.

While the garret suffered severe damage from air raids during the Second World War, the main part of the house survived virtually intact, much to everyone's amazement, considering that nearby Fetter Lane was reduced to rubble.

Touring the simply furnished house where Johnson lived from 1748 to 1759 with its curator, Betty Gathergood (three generations of her family have been curators here since the museum opened), one is delighted to be invited to make the acquaintance of a man about whom the Earl of Cork and Orrey noted,

THE PARLOR IS WHERE VISITORS WOULD HAVE BEEN SHOWN BEFORE BEING RECEIVED
BY DR. JOHNSON, WHOSE PORTRAIT (A CANVAS COPY BY MARGARET GRASE AFTER REYNOLDS)
HANGS ABOVE THE DISPLAY CASE. ON THE TABLE IS A THIRD EDITION OF
JOHNSON'S FAMOUS *DICTIONARY* OF 1755, WHICH FOR THE NEXT HUNDRED YEARS,
WOULD BE THE STANDARD WORK ON THE ENGLISH LANGUAGE.

"If you were a friend of his, you had no need of a library or a dictionary."

One of the main elements that renders a visit to Dr. Johnson's House so pleasurable is that its admirable restoration, as well as its collection of period furniture, books (including two first editions of the *Dictionary*), letters, period prints, mezzotints, portraits, and memorabilia, bring to life the man who was the subject of the finest biography in the English language, and who made such an indelible mark on English letters.

Johnson and his wife Elizabeth (who was affectionately nicknamed "Tetty") chose this house because of its proximity to William Strahan, the *Dictionary*'s printer. When they married in 1735, Johnson was twenty-five and his wife forty-six, a widow with three children. Many

contemporaries wondered why an attractive widow with a small fortune should marry a penniless young man, blind in one eye and scarred with scrofula, yet it proved to be a love match on both sides. While the actor David Garrick described her cruelly, "with swelled cheeks of florid red, produced by thick painting and increased by liberal use of cordials," Johnson was taken by her mass of soft blonde hair and her lively brown eyes, and said that she read comedy better than anyone he knew. When she died in 1752 at Gough Square, Johnson's grief was profound. For the rest of his life, he kept her wedding ring in a little wooden box, and remembered her in his prayers.

In the parlor is a portrait by an unknown artist (possibly a copy of a work by Joshua Reynolds) of Francis ("Frank") Barber, the former

Jamaican slave, who became Johnson's servant and principal heir. He came to Gough Square in 1752 and, apart from two intervals, stayed on until his master's death. Johnson sent Barber away to school and wrote him, "I am well satisfied with your progress. . . . Let me know what English books you read for your entertainment. You can never be wise unless you love reading."

Also on view is a third edition of the famous *Dictionary,* first published in 1755, which represents a feat of astonishing scholarship: 40,000 words are defined, and 114,000 quotations are cited demonstrating their usage. Johnson set a precedent in being the first lexicographer to systematically define words in what has become the standard method of classified sub-definitions. Prior to his work, dictionaries mainly defined words with synonyms.

Besides providing the etymology of the word and its definitions, Johnson

used quotations from such notable authors as Ben Jonson, John Milton, Alexander Pope, John Dryden, and William Shakespeare. An outstanding Greek and Latin scholar, as well as fluent in French and Italian, he did almost all the research himself, only using the Macbean brothers to help him with the Scottish and Gaelic analogies. When his physician Dr. William Adams expressed disbelief that the *Dictionary* could be completed within a period of three years (as Johnson estimated), noting that the French Academy with its forty members had taken forty years to compile its *Dictionary,* Johnson retorted: "Sir, thus it is. This is the proportion. Let me see; 40 times 40 is 1600. As three to 1600, so is the proportion of an Englishman to a Frenchman." (In actual fact, he was to underestimate the herculean task, which would ultimately take seven years.)

Sharp wit and caustic humor were often the hallmark of Johnson's definitions. For instance, he defined the word "lexicographer" as "a harmless drudge, that busies himself in tracing the original, and detailing the signification of words." He defined "pension" as "an allowance made to anyone without an equivalent. In England, it is generally understood to mean pay given to a state hireling for treason to his country." (Still, Johnson did accept an honorary pension of 300 pounds a year from George III, which freed him from his often besetting monetary troubles.)

Johnson compiled his famous *Dictionary* in the garret, employing six clerks to help him. In *The Life of Johnson,* James Boswell describes how "he had an upper room fitted up like a counting-house for the purpose" with a long desk at which several people could write standing. "The words, partly taken from other dictionaries, and partly supplied by himself, having been first written down with spaces left between them, he delivered in writing their etymologies, definitions and various significations. The authorities were copied from the books themselves, in which he had marked the passages with a black-lead pencil, the traces of which could be easily effaced."

Visiting 17 Gough Square, one is struck by the talented company with which Johnson associated for much of his life, including the painters Sir Joshua Reynolds and his sister Frances Reynolds, Elizabeth Carter, the noted translator of the Greek Stoic philosopher Epictetus, the novelist Frances Burney, and Elizabeth Montagu, "the Queen of the Blues," whose evening parties were attended by intellectual women, who wore stockings of blue worsted and who preferred learned conversation to playing cards.

It seems a pity that one cannot go back in time to partake in a lively conversation with this highly entertaining man, who often exchanged quips with his chronicler, Boswell, who was forever trying to persuade Johnson to accompany him on an excursion to his native Scotland. "Come sir," Boswell asked, "Do you not think that Scotland is worth seeing?" "Worth seeing, perhaps," Johnson conceded. "But not worth *going* to see."

The more one learns about Samuel Johnson, the more one is compelled to admire his wide-ranging mind and unflagging good nature. Despite being plagued by debt, illness, and depression, he seems to have been continually mindful of the welfare of others. When Oliver Goldsmith's landlady had him arrested for not paying his rent, it was Johnson who saved the day by selling Goldsmith's manuscript of *The Vicar of Wakefield* to a bookseller for

THE *DICTIONARY* WAS COMPILED IN THIS GARRET, WHERE JOHNSON EMPLOYED SIX CLERKS (FIVE OF WHOM WERE SCOTS) TO HELP HIM IN THE COMPILATION. EVEN IN THOSE DAYS, THE EXPENSE OF PREPARING SUCH A WORK WAS CONSIDERABLE, AND IT WAS A SYNDICATE OF BOOKSELLERS WHO CONTRACTED WITH JOHNSON FOR ITS PRODUCTION. THE COST IN TODAY'S CURRENCY WOULD BE ABOUT 157,000 POUNDS, OR ABOUT $250,000.

sixty pounds. When the poetess Anna Williams (Tetty's friend and companion) went blind after an unsuccessful eye operation, he took her in and gave her a home for the rest of her life.

Deciding that he wanted to make a liberal provision for his devoted servant Francis Barber in his will, he asked Dr. Richard Brocklesby to recommend a suitable annuity. When Brocklesby advised that a nobleman would consider fifty pounds a year adequate reward for many years of faithful service, Johnson replied: "Then I shall be *nobilissimus,* for I mean to leave Frank seventy pounds a year."

Of course, Johnson's greatest legacy was the *Dictionary,* which has had an inestimable impact on English language and literature. And a visit to Dr. Johnson's House at Gough Square makes it possible to better appreciate the prodigiously energetic and humanistic man who produced it.

ALTHOUGH THERE WERE ALWAYS
TWO DISTINCT RESIDENCES,
THE VIEW FROM THE ENTRANCE GATE
GIVES THE IMPRESSION OF
A SINGLE HOUSE.
THE PLUM TREE IN THE FOREGROUND
WAS PLANTED TO COMMEMORATE
THE ORIGINAL TREE UNDER WHICH
THE INSPIRED KEATS COMPOSED
HIS FAMOUS *ODE TO A NIGHTINGALE*.

Keats House

Wentworth Place
Keats Grove, Hampstead
London NW3 2RR
Tel: 0171–435–2062

Open Monday through Friday
10:00 A.M. to 1:00 P.M.
and 2:00 P.M. to 6:00 P.M.;
Saturday 10:00 A.M. to 1:00 P.M.
and 2:00 P.M. to 5:00 P.M.;
Sunday 2:00 P.M. to 5:00 P.M.
April to October.
Open Monday through Friday
1:00 P.M. to 5:00 P.M.;
Saturday 10:00 A.M. to 1:00 P.M.
and 2:00 P.M. to 5:00 P.M.;
Sunday 2:00 P.M. to 5:00 P.M.
November to March.

Bus: 24 to Hampstead Heath,
then walk two blocks to
Wentworth Place.

My heart aches, and a drowsy
numbness pains
My sense, as though of hemlock I
had drunk,
Or emptied some dull opiate to
the drains
One minute past, and Lethe-
wards had sunk:
'Tis not through envy of thy
happy lot,
But being too happy in thine
happiness—
That thou, light-winged Dryad
of the trees,
In some melodious plot
Of beechen green, and shadows
numberless,
Singest of summer in full-
throated ease.

THE poet John Keats (1795–1821) wrote these immortal lines from *Ode to a Nightingale* in the garden of the house he shared with his friend Charles Brown in the secluded village of Hampstead. In his memoirs, Brown told of how the sickly twenty-four-year-old poet came to compose the poem: "In the spring of 1819, a nightingale had built her nest near my house. Keats felt a tranquil and continual joy in her song, and one morning he took his chair from the breakfast table to the grass-plot under a plum tree where he sat for two or three hours. When he came into the house, I perceived he had some scraps of paper in his hand, and these he was quietly thrusting behind the books. On inquiry I found those scraps, four or five in number, contained his poetical feeling on the song of our nightingale."

OVER THE MANTELPIECE IN KEATS'S SITTING ROOM
IS A COPY OF JOSEPH SEVERN'S PAINTING *KEATS AT WENTWORTH PLACE,*
COMPLETED IN ROME (1821–23),
WHICH PORTRAYS THE POET IN HIS OWN WORDS:
"AND THERE I'D SIT AND READ ALL DAY LIKE A PICTURE OF SOMEBODY READING."
KEATS'S FRIEND CHARLES BROWN PROVIDED SEVERN WITH
THE ROOM'S DESCRIPTION,
A RECORD THAT HAS INSPIRED THE PRESENT ARRANGEMENT.

Today one can visit the Hampstead house and garden where Keats wrote many of his finest odes and sonnets, and find a fledgling plum tree commemorating the very spot where he heard the nightingale that inspired his famous ode. Although the Regency house was originally composed of two semi-detached residences, one occupied by Charles Wentworth Dilke, a civil servant and literary critic, and the other by Charles Brown, the view from the entrance gate has always given the impression of a single dwelling. This effect was achieved by placing the door to Brown's house (now known as the Keats-Brown house) at the side of the building and the door to Dilke's house centrally at the front.

After Keats's brother Tom died of tuberculosis in December 1818, Brown, a retired businessman and author, invited the poet to live with him at his home in Wentworth Place, Hampstead, already famed for its fresh air and idyllic landscape. Keats's share of Brown's house consisted of an upstairs bedroom and a sitting room, which remains much as it was. The sitting room's shutters on the French windows leading into the garden are still secured at night with the same stout iron bar the poet once used. This room also contains the bookcases where Keats kept his books

THE BRAWNE ROOMS, WHERE KEATS MET HIS FIANCÉE FANNY BRAWNE,
WERE MOST LIKELY TWO PARLORS WITH COMMUNICATING DOORS.
THE PORTRAIT OF THE PENSIVE AND YEARNING POET
BY WILLIAM HILTON R.A. WAS PROBABLY PAINTED IN 1822
FOR RICHARD WOODHOUSE,
A READER FOR TAYLOR AND HESSEY, KEATS'S PUBLISHERS.
THE HEPPLEWHITE DINING TABLE ONCE BELONGED TO THE POET
AND CRITIC LEIGH HUNT.

and where he hid the *Ode to a Nightingale,* which Brown was to discover and save from oblivion.

"Apart from his financial difficulties and a constant sore throat," notes curator Christina Gee, "the spring and summer of 1819 were probably the happiest period of Keats's short life. During this period five of his six great odes were written: *To Psyche, On Indolence, On Melancholy, To a Nightingale,* and *On a Grecian Urn.* At this time, he also wrote *Lamia, La Belle Dame sans Merci* and other sonnets."

"Charles Brown assiduously copied all the poems he could find and it is due to him and to another friend of

Keats, Richard Woodhouse (1788–1834), a reader for the publisher of Taylor and Hessey, that so much has been preserved that might otherwise have been lost."

In 1839, after Eliza Chester (1795–1859), a retired actress, acquired Wentworth Place, openings were made in the party wall so that the two properties were converted into a single house. The daughter of a market gardener who took up acting at the age of nineteen, Chester became mistress to the Prince Regent (the future King George IV) who fell in love with her and appointed her "Court Reader" at the substantial salary of six hundred pounds a year.

IT WAS IN THIS BEDROOM
THAT KEATS PREDICTED HIS IMMINENT
DEATH TO HIS FRIEND BROWN,
AFTER SEEING DROPS OF BLOOD HE HAD
SPIT UP ON THE BED SHEETS.
"I KNOW THE COLOR OF THAT BLOOD,"
HE EXCLAIMED,
"IT IS ARTERIAL BLOOD—I CANNOT BE
DECEIVED IN THAT COLOR . . .
—IT IS MY DEATH WARRANT
—I MUST DIE."

Percy Bysshe Shelley, the painter Joseph Severn (who accompanied him on his final journey to Rome), and the publisher John Taylor, who extolled the poet's gifts, there is also the notoriously damning review of *Endymion* by John Gibson Lockhart. Published in the August 1818 edition of *Blackwood's Review,* it snidely advised: "It is a better and a wiser thing to be a starved apothecary than a starved poet; so back to the shop, Mr. John, back to the 'plasters, pills and ointment boxes,' &c. But, for Heaven's sake, young Sangrado, be a little more sparing of extenuatives and soporifics in your practice than you have been in your poetry."

John Wilson Croker's slam in the influential *Quarterly* was even more cruel. "There is hardly a complete couplet enclosing a complete idea in the whole book," he excoriated, adding that *Endymion* was just another effusion of Cockney verse—"which may be defined to consist of the most incongruous ideas in the most uncouth language."

It was during this painful period that the diminuitive Keats (he was five feet one) met the equally petite eighteen-year-old Fanny Brawne in the front parlor of Wentworth Place. (Coincidentally, Fanny and her family lived at Wentworth Place briefly while Brown and Keats were away in Scotland, which makes it all the more fitting that her possessions should be displayed here.) By the summer of 1819, Keats and Fanny had become engaged. Visitors can see the engagement ring set with an almandite, a type of garnet, that Keats gave her, and that she wore until her death. Next to it is a delicate gold brooch in the form of a Greek lyre, with strings made of Keats's fair hair, a present intended for Fanny, but never given to her.

Chester also added a drawing room with a conservatory (renamed the Chester Room, it contains the bulk of the Keats collection), where she continued the literary heritage of the house, hosting such authors as William Makepeace Thackeray and Charles Dickens.

While almost two centuries have passed since Keats lived here, the house's simple yet elegantly furnished rooms convey a warmth and intimacy suggesting the poet is still very much in residence, surrounded by his favorite books, his letters, and some of his precious manuscripts, as well as such personal possessions as his writing-desk, his inkstand with the bust of Shakespeare, the medical notebook he kept as a student at the United Hospitals of Guy's and St. Thomas's (although he trained to be a doctor, he never practiced medicine), and the three first editions of his poems.

In addition to the wealth of memorabilia from friends and admirers, including the poets Leigh Hunt and

During the winter of 1819–20, Keats prepared his final volume, *Lamia, Isabella, The Eve of St. Agnes and Other Poems* for the press. These were months filled with frustration and disappointment. Poetry had rewarded him neither materially nor critically, his financial affairs were jeopardized by a lawsuit, and he seriously considered returning to medicine. Fortunately, the ever loyal Brown loaned him enough money to continue writing.

It was in Keats's reconstructed upstairs bedroom that the poet pronounced his own death sentence on February 3, 1820. When he returned chilled and fevered from riding on the outside of a coach from London, Brown persuaded him to go to bed. "Before his head was on the pillow," Brown recalls, "he slightly coughed, and I heard him say, 'That is blood from my mouth.' . . . After regarding it steadfastly, he looked up in my face with a calmness of countenance I can never forget and said, 'I know the color of that blood—it is arterial blood—I cannot be deceived in that color—that drop of blood— it is my death warrant—I must die.' " It was now certain that Keats had pulmonary tuberculosis.

Advised by his doctors that his only hope was to winter in Italy, he left Wentworth Place on September 13, 1820, and set off four days later with Severn for Rome. As England faded from sight, he transcribed in his copy of Shakespeare's *Poems,* his own sonnet *Bright Star* (the last poem he ever wrote) which begins:

Bright Star, would I were
steadfast as thou art—.

Visiting this loving memorial to English Romantic poetry, one senses Keats's last wish was granted, knowing how his incomparable poetry continues to stir and move the world. After seeing Wentworth Place, one begins to understand how Thomas Hardy came to write these stirring lines in *At a House in Hampstead* on the centenary of the poet's death:

Pleasanter now it is to hold
That here, where sang he,
more of him
Remains than where he,
tuneless, cold
Passed to the dim.

AMONG THE MOST IMPRESSIVE OBJECTS AT KEATS HOUSE ARE THE POET'S WRITING-DESK, HIS LIFE MASK, MADE BY BENJAMIN ROBERT HAYDON (WHILE HAYDON WAS PAINTING *CHRIST'S ENTRY INTO JERUSALEM*), HIS BELOVED INKSTAND WITH ITS BUST OF SHAKESPEARE, AND HIS PRIZED SHAKESPEARE FOLIO CONTAINING THE MANUSCRIPT OF HIS LAST SONNET, *BRIGHT STAR.*

Kenwood House, The Iveagh Bequest

Hampstead Lane
London NW3 7JR
Tel: 0181–348–1286

Open every day 10:00 A.M.
to 6:00 P.M. April 1 through
September 30; 10:00 A.M. to
4:00 P.M. October 1 through
March 31. Closed Christmas
Eve and Christmas Day.
Spring recitals in the Orangery;
outdoor summer concerts
mid-June to the beginning of
September. Concert inquiry
number: 0171–973–3427

Underground: Take the Northern
Line to either Golder's Green or
Archway, then take the 210 Bus
to Hampstead Lane, opposite the
East Lodge entrance.

Brew House Restaurant on the
premises.

In 1764, William Murray, the first Earl of Mansfield (1705–1793), commissioned the noted Scottish architect Robert Adam to remodel his Queen Anne stucco-covered brick villa on a splendid estate located in outer London between the fashionable spa town of Hampstead and the suburbs of Highgate. Mansfield, a noted aesthete and bibliophile, as well as a protégé of the poet Alexander Pope, was considered one of the greatest British barristers of his time. As Lord Chief Justice for thirty-two years, he not only reformed court procedure and amended commercial law to keep apace with the needs of an expanding empire, he also ruled against the rights of slaveholders over their slaves in England.

His choice of Adam was understandable: as the most eminent architect of the period, he had been

THE SOUTH FRONT OF KENWOOD HOUSE—OFTEN COMPARED TO A WEDDING CAKE—
STANDS ON THE CREST OF A RIDGE LINKING THE VILLAGES OF HAMPSTEAD AND HIGHGATE
AND COMMANDS A SPLENDID VIEW OF CENTRAL LONDON. THE HOUSE WAS
REMODELED BY ROBERT ADAM BETWEEN 1764 AND 1779, WHO ADDED A THIRD STORY,
PLUS THE WING CONTAINING HIS MAGNIFICENT LIBRARY, OR GREAT ROOM.

appointed joint Architect of the King's Works in 1761. Adam's designs fused a new lightness and "movement" into the weightier British Palladian architecture by incorporating elements from sixteenth-century Italian decoration and eighteenth-century French Rococo. Part of the pleasure of a visit to Kenwood House is the opportunity it affords the visitor to discover the first complete example of Adam's mature style, in both its exterior and interior aspects.

To the original brick house built around 1700, Adam added the imposing yet graceful wood portico on the north front (inspired by the Erechtheion on the Athenian Acropolis), as well as a third story, and the wing containing his awesome library, or Great Room. He then encased the entire structure in creamy white stucco and proceeded to decorate and furnish the interior, thus imbuing the house with his highly personal interpretation of the Neoclassical style.

Approaching the south front of the villa today, one cannot help but be struck by its dazzling white expanse, which dominates the crest of a ridge. The house commands a spectacular view of verdant meadows, a man-made lake, and a unilateral white sham bridge intended to create the illusion of a flowing river in the distance. Even with the skyscrapers of London dotting the horizon, the grounds of Kenwood suggest an idyllic arcadian setting. Strolling through the elegant and airy rooms of this eighteenth-century villa, one sees why it is an appropriate backdrop for its greatest treasure—a magnificent collection of paintings (bequeathed by Lord Iveagh to the nation in 1927), which includes

THE SHAM BRIDGE SPANNING THE MAN-MADE LAKE COMPLETES THE ILLUSION OF THE FLOWING RIVER AND EVOKES MEMORIES OF LANDSCAPE PAINTINGS BY CLAUDE LORRAIN AND NICOLAS POUSSIN.

such world-famous works as a late *Self-Portrait* by Rembrandt, *The Guitar Player* by Vermeer, and *Mary, Countess Howe* by Gainsborough, as well as fine paintings by Hals, Van Dyck, Reynolds, Romney, and Turner.

While Kenwood may not convey the same sense of grandeur as Osterley Park or Syon (Robert Adam's other great showplaces in outer London), few would dispute the architectural achievement and magnificence of the villa's Great Room, considered by many connoisseurs to be one of the architect's finest interiors. Adam, who sought to bring about "a kind of revolution in the whole system of architecture,"

drew his inspiration for this room from the Mausoleum in the Palace of Emperor Diocletian at Split, a seaport on the Adriatic coast in southern Croatia.

The first thing one is struck by is this library's unusual shape: a double cube with two semicircular apses and a cove ceiling. Adam's "revolution" is epitomized in this ceiling: its flat trunk is decorated with paintings by the Venetian Antonio Zucchi and fine stucco work by Joseph Rose, while the grounds of the panels and friezes are painted pastel shades of pink and blue—a marked contrast to the plain white ceilings of conventional Palladian interiors. While much has changed since the first Earl of

THE LIBRARY, OR GREAT ROOM, IS ONE OF THE
MOST SIGNIFICANT BRITISH EIGHTEENTH-CENTURY INTERIORS,
AND A MAJOR EXAMPLE OF NEOCLASSICAL ARCHITECTURE
AND INTERIOR DESIGN.
THE MIRRORED RECESSES ON THE NORTH WALL
REFLECT THE SPLENDID VIEW ON THE SOUTH LAWN.

THE MUSIC ROOM, THE SECOND MOST IMPORTANT ROOM AFTER THE LIBRARY,
CONTAINS MANY NOTABLE ENGLISH PORTRAIT PAINTINGS
(INCLUDING EXAMPLES BY GEORGE ROMNEY AND JOSHUA REYNOLDS),
AS WELL AS A CHAMBER ORGAN BY JOHN ENGLAND & SON (C. 1790),
SIMILAR TO THE ONE THAT ORIGINALLY GRACED THE ROOM.
IN FULL WORKING ORDER, THE ORGAN IS PLAYED AT OCCASIONAL RECITALS.

Mansfield entertained here such prominent guests as George III and Queen Charlotte, one can readily picture this magnificent room during a reception, aglow with candlelight from the candelabra, and with the firelight reflected off the mirrors and gilding.

Despite his marriage into the English aristocracy and his efforts to adopt an English accent and elocution, the "silver-tongued Murray" was not universally well-liked, and was suspected of being both a Papist and a Scottish Jacobite. (This was understandable, since both his father and brother had been imprisoned for taking part in the Jacobite rebellion of 1715, whose aim was to place James Edward Stuart on the throne.) During the anti-Popery Gordon Riots in 1780, Murray's London town house was sacked and reduced to ashes. Thanks to the swift and clever

ADAM'S VERSATILITY AS A DESIGNER IS SHOWN
IN THIS CHIMNEYPIECE IN THE UPPER HALL (C. 1773),
NOTABLE FOR ITS CARVED DECORATION
OF MERMEN FLANKED BY FLYING GRIFFINS AND
A CHERUB RIDING ON A SHELL DRAWN BY SEA HORSES.

action of David Murray, seventh Viscount Stormont (his nephew and heir), Kenwood was able to narrowly escape the same fate.

As the minister responsible for controlling the riots, Viscount Stormont ordered "a detachment of light horse" to intercept the mob that was advancing on the villa. As luck would have it, the landlord of the nearby Spaniard's Inn (still in existence today) succeeded in making

the rioters insensible with free ale— a move that was aided and abetted by Lord Mansfield's steward, who filled tubs with the brew from his master's cellar and set them out by the roadside.

Upon inheriting Kenwood, Viscount Stormont (1727–1796) commissioned the architect George Saunders to add two more wings to the main house, thereby expanding Adam's reception suite to the north, and providing the villa with a dining room and a music room, each with its own antechamber or lobby. Compared with Adam's magnificent portico entrance, the façade of the two Saunders wings (made of white Suffolk bricks) appears almost austere. The same simplicity and lack of gaudy ornamentation prevails in his interiors, even in his architectural tour-de-force in the lobby off the dining room, exemplified by the delicate plaster decoration in the robin's egg blue-and-white coffered ceiling, with its circular balustrade balcony and skylight overhead.

What makes this unusual museum especially worth a detour is its extraordinary collection of seventeenth-century Dutch and Flemish art, as well as many fine examples of British art of the late eighteenth century. In 1886, Guinness Breweries, the largest brewery in the world, became a public company, thus making Edward Cecil Guinness a multi-millionaire at the age of forty-three. (He was ennobled Earl of Iveagh and Viscount Elveden in 1919.) The following year he began to amass a collection of paintings through one Bond Street gallery, Agnews. Lord Iveagh's long-standing association with this gallery was quite accidental: after having been rebuffed by another gallery, which had refused to show him any pictures during his lunch-hour stroll, the considerably piqued collector was delighted to find Agnews more accommodating, and purchased two pictures on the spot: *The Flower Gatherers* by François Boucher and *View of Dordrecht* by Aelbert Cuyp. His relationship with Agnews flourished to such an extent that, within four years, Lord Iveagh had acquired some 240 paintings and drawings to furnish his vast town house in Grosvenor Place, Mayfair.

Despite the amount of advice he received from various experts as he put together his collection, Lord Iveagh ultimately followed his own taste and credos. The sixty-three paintings at Kenwood include a small group of French works from the Rococo period, an impressive assemblage of portraits and landscapes from the Dutch and Flemish schools, primarily from the seventeenth century, and an extensive selection of British portraits from the second half of the eighteenth century, mainly of great society beauties, including Lord Nelson's mistress, Lady Hamilton, and the famed actress, Mrs. Jordan (who bore William IV ten children out of wedlock, only to be brutally discarded when the monarch decided to marry Queen Charlotte).

THIS DISPLAY OF STUNNING EIGHTEENTH-CENTURY SILVER AND PASTE BUCKLES WAS BEQUEATHED BY LADY MAUFE (1884–1976) TO KENWOOD HOUSE. NOT ONLY DO THESE DOCUMENT THE CHANGES IN FASHION BEFORE THE ADVENT OF LACED FOOTWEAR, BUT THEY REPRESENT A FASCINATING VARIETY OF MATERIALS AND TECHNIQUES.

ROBERT ADAM'S GREAT STAIRS WERE INTENDED TO BE ADMIRED
BY GUESTS AS THEY WENDED THEIR WAY TO THE GREAT ROOM.
THE OPEN WROUGHT-IRON BALUSTRADE WITH ITS HONEYSUCKLE MOTIF,
THE MAHOGANY HANDRAIL, AND THE CARVED STAIRCASE
REMAIN UNCHANGED FROM THEIR ORIGINAL CONSTRUCTION.

To many connoisseurs, Kenwood's most extraordinary masterpiece is Jan Vermeer's *The Guitar Player* (a late work said to be a portrait of the artist's daughter at around sixteen), which his widow was forced to sell to pay off the family's bread debt. This exquisite painting (the only Vermeer in the country outside the National Gallery and the Royal Collection) was almost lost to the nation when it was stolen from Kenwood in 1974. Fortunately, thanks to assistance from a clairvoyant, the painting was found three months later, in Saint Bartholomew's Churchyard in Smithfield.

When Lord Iveagh died in 1927, he was reported to be the second richest man in the British Isles. The duties levied on his estate were such that Winston Churchill, then Chancellor of the Exchequer, was able to lower the nation's standard level of income tax. Lord Iveagh's fortune and munificence continue to benefit the country today, as exemplified by the delights of an outing to Kenwood, which offers visitors a chance to discover a jewel in English Neoclassical architecture, as well as an art collection that stands among the foremost in the nation.

Kettle's Yard

Castle Street
Cambridge CB3 OAQ
Tel: 01223–352124

House open Tuesday through
Sunday 2:00 P.M. to 4:00 P.M.
Gallery open Tuesday through
Saturday 12:30 P.M. to 5:30 P.M.;
Sunday 2:00 P.M. to 5:30 P.M.
September to Easter.
House open Tuesday through
Saturday 1:30 P.M. to 4:30 P.M.;
Sunday 2:00 P.M. to 4:30 P.M.
Easter to end of August.

Disabled Access to gallery and
with prior notice to the house,
including all concerts.

- **By train: Leave from King's Cross**
  or Liverpool Street Station; at
  Cambridge take bus 2, 6, 155,
  or 157 either to Trinity Street or
  Market Square.
- **By car: Take the M11 Exit 13,**
  then Madlingly Road to
  Northhampton Street. (The
  museum is on the corner of
  Northhampton and Castle
  Streets.)

IT has become commonplace to assume that outstanding public collections of modern art are to be found solely in formal museums. That is why it may come as quite a surprise to discover in a handsome and unpretentious house, known as Kettle's Yard (an hour by train outside of London, in the heart of Cambridge), paintings and sculptures by Ben and Winifred Nicholson, Henry Moore, Henri Gaudier-Brzeska, Juan Miro, Constantin Brancusi, William Cogden, and Barbara Hepworth.

Kettle's Yard is the brainchild of the art critic and author Jim Ede, who strongly believed that, in order for modern art to be properly appreciated and understood, an intimate environment was required where it could be shown, discussed and considered. "It was . . . in 1954 that I found myself dreaming of the idea of somehow creating a living space where works of art would be enjoyed, inherent to the domestic

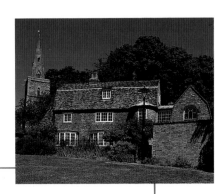

THIS HANDSOME BUILDING, KNOWN AS KETTLE'S YARD, WAS CREATED OUT OF
FOUR CONDEMNED SLUM DWELLINGS BEGINNING IN 1957 BY JIM EDE.
A FORMER CURATOR AT THE TATE GALLERY, EDE WANTED TO SHARE WITH OTHERS
THE ART AND OBJECTS HE HAD COLLECTED OVER FIFTY YEARS OR MORE,
IN WHAT HE CALLED "A CONTINUING WAY OF LIFE."

IN THE EXTENSION OF THE GREEN ROOM,
THE FAR WALL IS HUNG WITH BLACK-AND-WHITE ABSTRACT COLLAGES
BY THE ITALIAN ARTIST ITALO VALENTI (B. 1912),
WHILE THE SIDE WALLS DISPLAY WORKS BY BEN NICHOLSON AND
HENRI GAUDIER-BRZESKA, AMONG OTHERS.

setting, where young people could be at home unhampered by the greater austerity of the museum or public art gallery and where an informality might infuse an underlying formality," Ede explains in his book *A Way of Life*. "I wanted, in a modest way, to use the inspiration I had had from beautiful interiors, houses of leisured elegance; and to combine it with the joy I had felt in individual works seen in museums, with the all-embracing delight I had experienced in nature; in stones, in flowers, in people. These thoughts were greatly encouraged by American action, by the Phillips Memorial Gallery and by Dumbarton Oaks; homes made public and vital, by continued enterprise."

Although he initially had hoped for a "Stately Home" in which to house his world-class art collection, in the end Ede had to settle for the use of four tiny condemned slum dwellings given to him by the Cambridge Preservation Society in 1957, which he then renovated and occupied with his family.

In 1966, Ede donated Kettle's Yard to Cambridge University. In May 1970, a large extension, designed by Sir Leslie Martin, was opened to provide further display space for the collection and an art history library. What set Kettle's Yard apart from other traditional art institutions was Ede's decision to keep "open house" every afternoon, thus fostering a tradition of dynamic interaction between students and the artworks on display. Writing in *The Fortnightly Magazine*, Robin Lister, a former Cambridge student, recalls the lively atmosphere of learning and discussion (still maintained today, thanks to volunteer docents): "By allowing visitors to discover in his house the same exciting sense of beauty he himself feels so intensely, when walking among the rooms he knows and loves so well, he seeks to enable them to infuse a richness into their daily lives."

The diverse collections at Kettle's Yard are a tribute to Ede's avant-garde yet faultless taste, which enabled him to recognize exceptional works of art, long before established critics began to appreciate their merit. While he missed his chance to acquire works by Chagall, Rousseau, and Matisse at rock-bottom prices when he was living in Paris between the wars, he was among the first to appreciate the talent of the British painter Ben Nicholson.

Ede met Ben Nicholson and his sister Winifred when he was an assis-

tant at the Tate Gallery. "Oddly enough I turned out to be one of Ben Nicholson's very few admirers at that time, and after he had tried to sell a painting for a year or so, he would tell me I could have it for the price of the canvas and frame, usually one to three pounds. . . . Many he would give me, and now that Kettle's Yard has been catalogued I find it has 44 works of his . . . ," he notes exultantly in *A Way of Life*. Not only are the Nicholson paintings particularly fine, but they are an invaluable guide in understanding the range of styles and development in this artist's work.

Similarly, Ede was the first to discover and value the work of French sculptor Henri Gaudier-Brzeska (1891–1915), long before this notable talent was recognized by the art establishment. In 1931, Ede published a best-selling biography about the artist, *Savage Messiah* (later

ON THE BALCONY EXTENSION JIM EDE HAS LOVINGLY ARRANGED ALONG THE WALL, NEXT TO A QUEEN ANNE BUREAU, WORKS BY THE ENGLISH PRIMITIVE PAINTER ALFRED WALLIS (1855–1942) AND A STRIKING ABSTRACT SCULPTURE TITLED *THREE PERSONAGES*, BY BARBARA HEPWORTH (FOREGROUND).

EDE HAD NO PROBLEM MIXING ANTIQUE BONE CHINA AND GLASS
WITH A BUDDHIST FIGURINE AND A METAL SCULPTURE
BY CONSTANTIN BRANCUSI (1876–1957).
EDE PURCHASED BRANCUSI'S *FISH* IN 1927, AT THE TIME THE ARTIST
WAS DEFENDING HIS WORKS IN THE UNITED STATES COURTS
TO KEEP THEM FROM BEING CLASSIFIED AS TAXABLE METAL.

made into a film by Ken Russell), based on letters the sculptor had written to his companion, Sophie Gaudier-Brzeska. How Ede was able to acquire the French sculptor's collection for virtually a pittance, so that Kettle's Yard now boasts the most comprehensive collection of his work, may go down as one of the greatest art coups of this century.

Recalling in *A Way of Life* how he came upon an extraordinary cache of Gaudier-Brzeska's work, he writes: "In [1926] I first heard of Gaudier-Brzeska. A great quantity of his work was dumped in my office at the Tate. It was 10 years after Gaudier's death, and all his work had been sent to many art experts for their opinion and London dealers had been asked to buy. It had become property of the Treasury. In the end I got a friend to

ABOUT THIS MANTELPIECE, EDE WRITES IN *A WAY OF LIFE*:
"HAD IT NOT BEEN FOR THE PAINTINGS OF [SALVADOR] DALI, I WOULD HAVE
KICKED THE SHELLS AWAY AS BROKEN AND KETTLE'S YARD
WOULD NEVER HAVE HAD THIS SO BEAUTIFUL COMBINATION OF FORMS."

buy *Chanteuse Triste* for the Tate. I subsequently gave three [works] to the Contemporary Art Society and three more to the Tate. It took some doing to persuade them to accept even this—and the rest for a song, I bought."

According to Roger Cole's biography, *Gaudier-Brzeska, Artist and Myth,* it took a series of adroit moves for Ede to acquire the remaining art collection for the sum of sixty pounds, including nineteen sculptures, as well as more than 1,500 drawings, pastels, oils, tools, and boxes of papers. Because of the Treasury's rule

that government property could not be sold to civil servants without sanction, Ede's friend, McKnight Kauffer, acted as his agent. Both men paid an additional thirty-five pounds for the copyright. Later, by making casts of some of Gaudier's sculptures, the originals of which he kept, Ede used his superb collection to begin the endowment fund for Kettle's Yard.

Strolling through the inviting, airy house, one is struck by Ede's unerring eye, which perceived how to marry the simple, handsome lines of Queen Anne furniture (the house

THIS STILL-LIFE ARRANGEMENT
OF SCULPTURE, FLOWERS, AND STONES
HAS NEVER WAVERED
FROM EDE'S ORIGINAL SCHEME.

contains a Queen Anne bureau that he purchased for eight pounds when he was twelve years old), with frayed Moroccan rugs, salvaged artisanal tools, colorful chipped pottery, shells, stones, and stunning works of art. Yet, more than anything else, one is struck by a pervasive serenity and harmony throughout, demonstrating that different styles and centuries of fine and decorative arts can coexist happily and naturally together.

Explaining his decision to donate Kettle's Yard to Cambridge, Ede writes in *A Way of Life:* "I have felt strongly the need for me to give again these things which have so much been given to me, and to give in such a way, that by their placing, and by a pervading atmosphere, one thing will enhance another, making perhaps a coherent whole; and where a continuity of enjoyment, in the constantly changing public of a university, has some chance to thrive, and from which other ventures of this sort may spring. There should be a Kettle's Yard in every university." Anyone who has the opportunity to visit this beautiful and exceptional collection is bound to agree wholeheartedly.

WHILE THE ARAB HALL
IS MEANT TO SUGGEST THE ARABIAN NIGHTS,
IT IS BY NO MEANS A SLAVISH COPY OF MIDDLE EASTERN
ARCHITECTURE, BUT RATHER A VISION
THAT WAS CONSONANT WITH VICTORIAN NOTIONS.
A BRONZE STATUETTE OF *NARCISSUS*
(A REPRODUCTION OF THE ONE IN THE NAPLES MUSEUM)
STANDS POISED ON THE PEDESTAL.

Leighton House Museum

**12 Holland Park Road
London W14 8LZ
Tel: 0171–602–3316**

**Open Monday through Saturday
11:00 A.M. to 5:30 P.M.**

**Underground: Take the District
Line to High Street Kensington
Bus: 9, 9A, 10, 27, 33, 49 to
Odeon Cinema/Commonwealth
Institute. The museum is north
of High Street Kensington, off
Melbury Road.**

FLUSHED with success from the sale of his painting *Dante in Exile* for one thousand guineas, in 1864 the independently wealthy and fashionable painter Frederic Leighton (1830–1896) commissioned architect George Aitchison to design an elegant studio-house on a plot of land in the western part of London (in an area known today as Holland Park). The site was ideal for an artist, since the prevailing winds blew the city's smog from west to east, thus affording the painter unsullied natural daylight.

Completed in 1866, Leighton's residence and studio was made of red Suffolk brick and ornamented

THE REAR OF LEIGHTON HOUSE,
WITH ITS RED SUFFOLK BRICK EXTERIOR
AND CENTRALLY PLACED STUDIO WINDOW,
OVERLOOKS A BRONZE STATUE TITLED
A MOMENT OF PERIL, WHICH WAS SCULPTED AND CAST
BY THOMAS BROCK IN 1880.

with cream Caen stone. With its centrally placed studio window facing north, the house was intended for a bachelor artist, with living quarters on the ground floor, and a studio, bedroom, and reception rooms on the second floor.

For thirty years, Leighton lived and worked here, settling on a Classical style of painting, which he had learned on the Continent (under the tutelage of artist Ary Scheffer), and to which he remained faithful for the rest of his life. A solitary man, he never married, insisting, "I am married to my art." (Overnight guests were not welcome at Leighton House, because they were thought to interfere with the artist's work.)

Despite his jealously guarded privacy, Leighton's friendship with the Prince of Wales resulted in his becoming a leading exponent of art in Britain, and gave him a pivotal role in the early development of such major institutions as the South Kensington Museum (now the Victoria and Albert Museum), the British Museum, and the Tate Gallery. In 1878, he was elected President of the Royal Academy and knighted, and in 1884 he was named a baron by Queen Victoria. During his final illness, he was made a peer, the only British artist to be thus honored.

In light of his active social schedule, Leighton required a home that was a public art gallery and

a salesroom, as well as a studio. Leighton House was all of these and more. Brimming over with Italian Renaissance statuettes and bas-reliefs, early Chinese bronze bowls and vases, seventeenth-century Dutch furniture, Persian rugs and prayer mats, English and Turkish silver, as well as Old Master drawings, the house's rich, dense atmosphere and assembly of beautiful objects reflected the artist's tastes and temperament. It also

IN 1895, LEIGHTON COMMISSIONED AITCHISON TO CREATE A SKYLIT
PICTURE GALLERY, KNOWN AS THE SILK ROOM,
(SO-CALLED BECAUSE OF ITS TAUPE-COLORED SILK HANGINGS),
IN WHICH PAINTINGS BY HIS CONTEMPORARIES COULD BE PROPERLY DISPLAYED,
INCLUDING JOHN EVERETT MILLAIS'S *SHELLING PEAS*.

provided him with an endless source of inspiration for the sort of academic painting that appealed so much to his Victorian patrons.

While Leighton was the first artist to move to Holland Park, he soon had as neighbors Val Prinsep, who lived on an adjoining plot, G.F. Watts, and Hamo Thornycroft. "The idea of the 'artist's house' proclaimed the owner to be different from his neighbors," wrote Leonée and Richard Ormond in *Lord Leighton*. "In place of the enlightened connoisseurs of earlier generations, it was the artists themselves who now became the arbiters of taste. Seen in this context, 2 Holland Park Road [the address at that time] was more than simply a home of a

practicing artist. It proclaimed the role which Leighton had assumed as a guardian of taste in an age of general philistinism."

Besides being a tastemaker, Leighton was also a generous and thoughtful host. His annual parties were attended by such celebrated guests as the Prince of Wales, Prime Minister William Gladstone, and novelist George Eliot, together with the finest musical talents of the period, including Clara Schumann, Pauline Viardot, and Sir Charles and Lady Hallé. One guest, Alice Corkran, recalled in her book, *Frederic, Lord Leighton,* how "splendid carpets hung from the gallery at one end of the studio, flowers of perfect bloom brightened every

THE EBONY STAIRCASE, STUFFED PEACOCK,
CORINTHIAN COLUMNS, AND MOORISH TILES
CONSPIRE TO MAKE AN ENCHANTING
ENTRANCE FOR GUESTS.

corner. The pictures of the year stood about on easels. Lovely and charming women, men distinguished in every walk of life, thronged the rooms . . . the house was filled with Joachim's and Piatti's violins, with the accent of perfect voices singing."

While such enthralling evenings are sadly no more, and Leighton's superb collection of Old Masters, furniture, and objets d'art was auctioned off after his death to satisfy the generous bequests in his will, a tour of the beautifully restored Leighton House Museum helps one to understand why Mrs. Russell Barrington orchestrated a campaign to save the house for the nation, claiming it was "as notable a creation in Art as any of Leighton's pictures or statues."

Entering the glass-roofed front hall, with its black-and-white mosaic flooring and stately ebony-wood staircase, one is immediately struck by the sight of a strutting stuffed peacock at the bottom of the steps and a huge potted palm—the two ubiquitous symbols of the Aesthetic movement. Equally impressive is Leighton's collection of pottery and the deep blue tiling on the stairs and in the adjacent anteroom. Made and installed in 1879–81 by the noted ceramicist William de Morgan, both the stoneware and tilework were inspired by the painter's magnificent collection of Syrian-Iznik ware and tiles.

The showpiece of Leighton House is indubitably the Arab Hall, designed and built by Aitchison from 1877–79. This two-story extension in the western part of the house was intended to accommodate Leighton's collection of pottery and tiles acquired on his travels to the Middle East. Aitchison based the hall's design loosely on the reception hall of the twelfth-century Muslim palace of La Zisa (The Palace of Delights), a room that was much admired and frequently drawn by nineteenth-century travelers.

The chief reception room in any substantial Arab house has a pool or fountain in the center, with raised alcoves at the sides, decorated in tile or mosaic. The Arab Hall and the hall in La Zisa share these features, together with a distinctive use of pillars at the corners of the room, and a similar type of pendentive dome.

SINCE THE REPRESENTATION
OF LIVING CREATURES
WAS BANNED BY ISLAMIC LAW
UNDER THE OTTOMAN EMPIRE,
THE BIRDS IN THIS PANEL
HAVE AT SOME DATE
HAD THEIR THROATS "CUT"
BY CHIPPING A LINE IN THE GLAZE,
SO AS TO MAKE THEM
THEOLOGICALLY ACCEPTABLE.

The walls are covered with tiled panels from Persia and Syria, framed by patterned borders, and a magnificent frieze containing verses from the Koran, brought back by Sir Richard Burton from one of the hill temples at Sind in northern India, now a province in southeastern Pakistan. (Burton, a close friend of Leighton's, was the first European to disguise himself as a Muslim pilgrim and go to Mecca.)

The Arab Hall was not an exact reconstruction, nor was it ever intended to be. Leighton and Aitchison worked with several leading designers so that the splendid room became a showplace of the period's decorative arts. Walter Crane designed the gilt mosaic frieze around the walls, Randolph Caldecott modeled the capitals of the marble columns at the hall's entrance, while Edgar Boehm carved the capitals of the alabaster columns flanking the sofas. William de Morgan arranged the late-sixteenth-and-seventeenth-century Syrian and Iznik tiles in the hall itself. Because many of the sets were incomplete and did not match, De Morgan had to do some ingenious infilling. The patchwork arrangement of the tiles is quite unlike anything to be found in an Arab domestic interior or in a mosque, where pervasive, repetitious patterns tend to be the norm.

"The Arab Hall, like the Turkish smoking room, was a nineteenth-century male preserve, where men would go after dinner to smoke their cigars," notes curator Julia Findlater. "It was very much a reflection of male culture and design at that time." On one occasion, after a dinner party attended by James McNeill Whistler, Edward Burne-Jones, and Albert Moore, one guest accidentally stepped right into the black marble fountain in the center of the room,

LEIGHTON COMMISSIONED WALTER CRANE
TO DESIGN THIS MOSAIC FRIEZE AROUND THE WALLS,
BASED ON A SIMILAR ONE IN THE PALACE
OF LA ZISA IN PALERMO, ITALY.

apparently disturbing two somnolent Japanese tench.

The hub of the house is the Pompeian red-walled studio, where Leighton painted and sold his work, some of which is still on display. The gilded domes and apse are the only elements left that convey an idea of the former luxury of the studio's appointments. "He kept it much like Rubens's studio," explains Findlater, "working simultaneously on as many as six paintings at once."

Leighton was such an intriguing artist and personality that he inspired fictional characters in novels by Henry James and Benjamin Disraeli. Touring his splendid home today, one can imagine him in the character of Mr.

Phoebus, as Disraeli did in his novel *Lothair.* "Mr. Phoebus liked pomp and graceful ceremony, and he was of the opinion that great artists should lead a princely life, so that in their manners and method of existence they might furnish a model to mankind in general, and elevate the tone and taste of nations." Now, as visitors appreciate the splendid preservation of this unusual home, they can discover the aesthetic universe of this eminent Victorian for themselves.

Museum of London

London Wall
London EC2Y 5HN
Tel: 0171–600–3699

Open Tuesday through Saturday
and Bank Holiday Mondays
10:00 A.M. to 5:50 P.M.;
Sunday Noon to 5:50 P.M.
(Last admission 5:30 P.M.)

Disabled Access.

Underground: Take the
Metropolitan or Circle Line to
Barbican, or the Central Line
to St Paul's Station.
Bus: Museum of London 4, 172,
279; St Paul's 8, 11, 15, 23, 25,
26, 501, 521

Museum café on premises.

MOST visitors to London who
fly in to Heathrow, the world's largest
airport, might be surprised to learn
that in 800 B.C. it was an important
prehistoric settlement containing
eleven large round mud dwellings
with circular thatched roofs and a
rectangular religious shrine. When the
site was first discovered and excavated
in 1944 to make way for Heathrow
Airport, it was oddly enough named
"Caesar's Camp," even though Julius
Caesar came to Britain in 55 B.C.,
the same year he invaded Gaul.

THIS EIGHTEENTH-CENTURY COSTUME CASE
ILLUSTRATES THE CITY'S CALICO TRADE;
ALL THE DRESSES ON DISPLAY
ARE MADE OF ENGLISH PRINTED LINEN,
(C. 1770–1785).

THESE PUNCH AND JUDY PUPPETS
WERE A POPULAR FEATURE AT STREET FAIRS
IN NINETEENTH-CENTURY LONDON.

Nor would most of London's residents and tourists suspect that the shape of the largest city in Europe was once defined by a massive city wall built by the Romans (c. A.D. 197–211), parts of which are still extant today, and which once provided the foundations for the city's medieval wall, built between 1066 and 1480. It seems that a cache of forged silver coins, some depicting the Roman Emperor Caracalla, along with several hundred forgers' molds, enabled local archaeologists to document the city's wall construction, as well as to demonstrate that as early as A.D. 213–217 the forging of coins was widespread.

THIS RECONSTRUCTED LIVING ROOM
IN A WEALTHY LONDON HOME (C. A.D. 300)
CONTAINS REPRODUCTION FURNITURE
AND ORIGINAL OBJECTS FROM ROMAN LONDON.

These are only a few of the fascinating discoveries awaiting visitors to the Museum of London, one of the foremost historical city museums in the world, yet one of the best-kept secrets of the capital. Located inside a modern building complex overlooking part of the city's ancient Roman and medieval wall, the museum's two levels of highly imaginative exhibition galleries trace the chronology of London from 500,000 B.C. right through to the present day. (While the museum recommends allowing a half-hour for viewing each gallery, not even an entire day can do justice to the scope of the exhibits.)

An ingenious use of dioramas, life-size models, artists' reconstructions, period artifacts, and piped-in sounds, re-create the environment faced by the first Britons, as they foraged for their survival across land now submerged under the English Channel. As the climate warmed and the glaciers retreated, small bands of people gathered plants for food and hunted animals, which included reindeer and red deer, evidence of which was uncovered at different sites in Uxbridge. Later, fields and farms were created in forest clearings such as those discovered at Runnymede. Domesticated animals, cereal crops, and the first pottery (pieces of which are on display), were already in evidence during this period (c. 500,000 B.C.–A.D. 43).

The curatorial staff has also taken great pains to provide some unexpected insights into the origins of British culture, such as the fact that Cornish and Welsh are descended from the pre-Roman language spoken by

THIS LATE STUART INTERIOR, WITH PANELING AND A CHIMNEYPIECE FROM POYLE PARK NEAR FARNHAM, SURREY, CAME FROM A LONDON MERCHANT FAMILY'S COUNTRY HOUSE. THE CARVING, IN AN "ARTISAN MANNERIST" STYLE (C. 1648–55), IS ALMOST CERTAINLY BY A LONDON CARPENTER.

native Britons, and that the names "London" and "Thames" are prehistoric in origin. Whereas most museums have a "don't touch" policy, here one can caress a piece of prehistory, such as a flint hand-ax from Yiewsley dated 350,000–120,000 B.C. and an early flat ax of copper (c. 2100–1900 B.C.), shown alongside their modern equivalents, and see how the tools one takes for granted have come down to us through the centuries.

Following the Roman invasion by troops of the Emperor Claudius in A.D. 43, a colony grew up on the north bank of the Thames. Together with a smaller settlement, south of the river (in what is now Southwark), the site became a useful depot for the Roman army, as well as for traders. However, the town was destroyed around A.D. 60 during the uprising of Queen Boudicca, and little is known of this early community. Around A.D. 100 London, or Londinium, was rebuilt and became the capital city of Britain, the most northern province of the Empire, a city that was to flourish for almost four hundred years. Local excavations have revealed a forum and basilica, a fort, an amphitheater, and public baths (many of which were decorated with elaborate mosaics and statuary), parts of which have been unearthed and put on display. The daily life of Roman London comes alive to present-day visitors through impressive re-creations of domestic interiors showing the lifestyle of the nouveau riche as well as the poor, and through rows of workshops (including those of glass and leather artisans and a cutler's stall). Many of the latter have been

THIS NINETEENTH-CENTURY BARBERSHOP
OFFERED A WIDE RANGE OF SERVICES,
INCLUDING WET AND DRY SHAMPOOING AND SINGEING.
MANY BARBERS RAN A TOILET CLUB
FOR REGULAR CUSTOMERS,
KEEPING MEMBERS' PERSONAL SHAVING EQUIPMENT
IN A SPECIAL CUPBOARD IN THEIR SHOPS.

THIS DUTCH SCHOOL OIL PAINTING ON OAK OF
THE GREAT FIRE OF LONDON 1666
SHOWS THE BLAZE AS IT WOULD HAVE APPEARED
FROM THE VIEWPOINT OF A BOAT
IN THE VICINITY OF TOWER WHARF;
ALTHOUGH THE WHARF DEPICTED IN THE FOREGROUND
NEVER EXISTED, THE GENERAL RENDERING OF
LONDON'S TOPOGRAPHY AND THE FIRE'S EFFECTS
ARE QUITE ACCURATE.

equipped with sound systems replicating the city's lively commerce.

Following the collapse of Rome, London was a sparsely populated ruin for two centuries during the period known as The Dark Ages. Anglo-Saxon immigrants from northern Germany settled in the countryside around London, bringing a new language—Old English—and driving out or intermarrying with native Britons. A new settlement, known as "Lundewic" grew up outside the ancient Roman city walls, westward along what is now the Strand, where longships could be easily beached. It became a center for foreign trade with France and the Rhineland, attracting Viking raiders from Scandinavia, so that by the beginning of the eleventh century most of eastern England, including London, was in the hands of Danish invaders, some of whose deadly battle-axes and spears are on display.

After the Norman Conquest in 1066, London grew in wealth and population during the Middle Ages and the Renaissance; with the Norman kings, other immigrants came to the city, among them were merchants from northern France and Jewish moneylenders. New stone buildings were erected, including the

Tower of London, London Bridge, and an imposing new St. Paul's Cathedral (England's largest cathedral until it was destroyed in the Great Fire of 1666). While trade and industry flourished, as evidenced by the fine displays of metalwork and fashionable garb (including shoes with pointed toes), the city was also subject to the bubonic plague in 1348–49. Known as the Black Death, it ravaged Europe—crude lead crosses on display point to the mass burials of the victims of this deadly disease.

The museum's most gripping exhibit is indubitably a diorama complete with dramatic light and sound effects that reenacts the Great Fire of London. Samuel Pepys, the city's noted diarist, recalled in vivid detail how the fire broke out on September 2, 1666, in the king's bakery in Pudding Lane, raged for four days and obliterated four-fifths of the city. Eighty-eight of the city's ninety seven parish churches were reduced to burned-out shells, including St. Paul's Cathedral, where only John Donne's monument remained intact. While over 100,000 Londoners were left homeless and were forced to camp out in open fields during the following winter, miraculously only eight people died. The parliamentary report on the fire's causes was succinct: "The hand of God upon us, a great wind, and a season so very dry."

Yet, in the face of this disaster, the inhabitants of London proved surprisingly resilient, and the city was

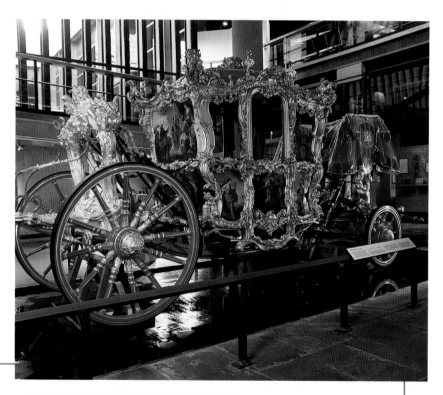

IN 1757, THE ALDERMEN OF THE CITY OF LONDON COMMISSIONED JOSEPH BERRY
TO BUILD "A NEW GRAND STATE COACH";
THIS MASTERPIECE OF ENGLISH ROCOCO COST SIX HUNDRED-AND-EIGHTY POUNDS
TO MANUFACTURE AND WAS COMPLETED IN SIX MONTHS.
IT HAS BEEN THE FOCAL POINT OF THE LORD MAYOR'S SHOW
EVER SINCE THE YEAR IT WAS MADE.

THE GROWING INTEREST IN SCIENCE IN SEVENTEENTH-CENTURY LONDON
IS DEMONSTRATED IN THIS DISPLAY CASE SHOWING SCIENTIFIC INSTRUMENTS
FROM THE PERIOD, INCLUDING A LANTERN CLOCK, A CIRCUMFERENTOR,
A COMPOUND MICROSCOPE, A TELESCOPE, A HORIZONTAL DIAL, AND A COMPASS.

rebuilt quickly. The museum shows that under both Charles II and James II, the city prospered from a stable economy and the benefits of applied science, with Royal Society members Robert Boyle and William Petry encouraging major developments in shipbuilding, cloth-dying, and steam pumps. London soon became a nationwide supplier of glass, Delft and stoneware pottery, as well as coaches. Moreover by 1685, many of the city's 15,000 Huguenot refugees were working in the luxury trades, producing fine textiles, watches, and other remarkable precision instruments, numerous examples of which are on display.

What makes a visit to the Museum of London so rewarding is that its extensive displays succeed not only in documenting the city's changing face over two thousand years, but also in re-creating everyday life, with its glaring contrasts of wealth and poverty, war and peace, of prosperous merchants and striking laborers, of sleek dandies and overworked dressmakers. Whether one is strolling past an elegant reconstructed room that conforms with the building regulations established after the Great Fire of 1666, or peering into a nineteenth-century reconstructed grocer's shop where the large painted canisters once held teas, and where paraffin used to be sold for household lighting and heating, London's indomitable, irrepressible spirit shines through, demonstrating in countless ways why it has inspired poets and writers for centuries, and why it has become and continues to be a mecca for so many people from around the world.

Florence Nightingale Museum

(St. Thomas's Hospital
at Car Park Level)
2 Lambeth Palace Road
London SE1
Tel: 0171–620–0374

Open Tuesday through Sunday
and Bank holidays 10:00 A.M.
to 5:00 P.M.
(Last admission 4:00 P.M.)

Disabled Access.

Underground: Take the Northern
Line to Waterloo Station or
Westminster.
Bus: C1, 12, 53, 109, 171, 171A,
211, 507, 511

THIS BRONZE CAST, TAKEN FROM
A MARBLE BUST OF
FLORENCE NIGHTINGALE
BY SIR JOHN STEELL,
WAS PRESENTED TO HER BY THE
NON-COMMISSIONED OFFICERS AND MEN
OF THE BRITISH ARMY IN 1862.
THE CAST WAS MADE BY A. PARLANTI
OF THE ARTISTIC FOUNDRY IN LONDON.

"EVERYONE knows the popular conception of Florence Nightingale. The saintly, self-sacrificing woman, the delicate maiden of high degree who threw aside the pleasures of a life of ease to succour the afflicted, the Lady with the Lamp, gliding through the horrors of the hospital at Scutari, and consecrating with the radiance of her goodness the dying soldier's couch—the vision is familiar to all. But the truth was different . . . a Demon possessed her. Now demons, whatever else they may be, are full of interest. And so it happens that in the real Miss Nightingale there was more that was interesting than in the legendary one; there was also less that was agreeable."

So wrote the noted biographer Lytton Strachey (1880–1932) in *Eminent Victorians* (1918). A visit to the award-winning museum devoted to the life and work of Florence Nightingale (1820–1910), within St. Thomas's Hospital, the very hospital where she founded the world's first school of nursing over a century ago, amply bears out his often quoted statement. Through personal artifacts, paintings, prints, photographs and sculpture, set-pieces, and quotations from Nightingale and her contemporaries, the museum presents this remarkable woman at successive stages in her life, from the privileged and well-educated child and young woman growing up on country estates at Lea Hurst, Derbyshire, and Embley Park, Hampshire, to the rebel who chose a life of service and reform. This indomitable spirit took on the tradition-bound British Army, and became the founder of the

Nightingale Training School for Nurses, as well as the author of over 200 books, pamphlets, and reports that revolutionized medical care at military and civilian hospitals, and the field of nursing itself.

Named after the Italian city, Florence received an unusually challenging education from her father, William Nightingale, that included the study of mathematics, algebra, philosophy, statistics, Latin and Greek, as well as French, German, and Italian. Although she admitted to having "the most enormous desire for acquiring" [knowledge], she nonetheless felt trapped by her social background and wealth. "I am up to my chin in linen and glass," she wrote to her friend Mary Clarke. "Is all that china, linen and glass necessary to make man a Progressive animal?"

To her mind, the answer was a resounding no, even to the point of rejecting marriage and traditional domesticity, much to the consternation of her family. Her compulsion to lead a life of constructive self-sacrifice

HERE IS THE MEDICINE CHEST
THAT FLORENCE NIGHTINGALE TOOK WITH HER TO
SCUTARI AT THE HEIGHT OF THE CRIMEAN WAR.

was concretized on February 7, 1837, when "God spoke to me and called me to His Service." Yet, the museum reveals that not until 1845 did she determine her calling, announcing to her parents her desire to work as a nurse at the Salisbury Infirmary. Her parents were appalled: "It was as if I wanted to be a kitchen maid." This was understandable, given the times. Not only were nurses often thought of as being drunken slatterns, but England's upper classes also had a strong prejudice against any work tainted by "service."

It would be another eight years before Florence would be able to actively pursue her vocation. In 1853, in the face of fierce family opposition, she left at last for Paris, visiting almshouses and medical institutions for a month, and acquiring as much information as possible about hospitals and nursing throughout Europe —a fact-finding mission that would later serve her well. Returning from this trip, she obtained a position as superintendent of a charitable institution caring for sick gentlewomen in Harley Street.

Nonetheless, she yearned to work in a real hospital, an opportunity that England's Secretary of War Sidney Herbert would provide for her the following year in a letter written on October 15, 1854—a watershed in her life: "Dear Miss Nightingale, You will have seen in the papers that there is a great deficiency of nurses at the Hospital at Scutari. . . ." Several days later, on October 21, Nightingale left with her party for the Crimea, arriving in Scutari on November 4. It was the height of the Crimean War. While the *Times* had declared that the British Army in the Crimea was "the finest army that ever left these shores," the reality was far different: most soldiers had never before seen active service, and the administration at every level was a nightmare. Shortly after her arrival, Nightingale wrote: "We are steeped up to our necks in blood. These poor fellows have not had a clean shirt nor have been washed for two months before they came here. We have not a basin nor a bit of towel nor a bit of soap nor a broom."

Undaunted by the stench, the filth, and the dying, or by the British Army's obdurate medical authorities (who thought she was asking for "preposterous luxuries" when she campaigned for clean clothes, bedding, and better food for patients), within a month Nightingale had transformed the barracks hospital at Scutari from a sinkhole of atrocity into a place of hope. Her accomplishments were monumental: reorganizing the kitchen for special medical diets, cleaning the wards, distributing 2,000 cotton and flannel shirts and organizing the washing, creating a lying-in hospital, and attending to the needs of the soldiers' wives and widows. In addition to improving the general level of cleanliness and sewage disposal, she made certain the wards were sufficiently repaired to accommodate an additional 800 wounded. Her dedication to the common soldier was astonishing: not only did she insist on inspecting the Crimean hospital in Balaclava, traveling in a converted baggage cart over snow and perilously uneven terrain, but she refused to leave the region "until every soldier has gone from Scutari Hospital."

What this fascinating museum makes quite clear is that Florence's achievements at Scutari were only a prelude to a life-long career dedicated to improving hospital conditions and the practice of medicine. Within six weeks of her much-acclaimed return from the Crimea, this fearless bundle of energy and resolve had embarked

ONE OF THE WARDS OF THE HOSPITAL AT SCUTARI IS A LITHOGRAPH FROM AN ENGRAVING
BY WILLIAM SIMPSON, PUBLISHED BY P & D COLNAGHI IN 1856.

THIS LIFE-SIZE RE-CREATED HOSPITAL WARD AT SCUTARI DEPICTS FLORENCE,
"THE LADY WITH THE LAMP," ATTENDING TO THE SICK
WHILE A MAN'S LEG IS BEING AMPUTATED.

on a program of Army reform with Sidney Herbert, aided by a small "Cabinet" of like-minded reformers. Queen Victoria was a warm supporter of her work, writing to the Duke of Cambridge, "I wish we had her at the War Office."

However, taking on the British Army was only one facet of her ambitious program. Realizing that her success in the Crimea had generated a new-found respect for the vital role of nursing, she helped spearhead a national fund-raising effort that netted 45,000 pounds within twenty months, enough money for her to "establish a permanent institution for the training, sustenance and protection of nurses and to arrange for their proper instruction."

While a number of hospitals were approached as possible locales for a school of nursing, it was the offer from St. Thomas's that was finally accepted. Thus the Florence Nightingale School of Nursing was established, which to this day bears her name. Its aim was nothing less than revolutionary: whereas nurses had previously focused on the spiritual well-being of patients, they would now be trained in the management of the sick and convalescents, make full use of their powers of observation to keep the medical staff informed of each patient's welfare, as well as attend to the hospital's overall cleanliness.

For twenty years after her return from the Crimea, Florence Nightingale devoted her life to medical reform: her achievements included improving the British Army's sanitary conditions at home and in India, planning military and civilian hospitals, and laying the foundations of modern nursing. She also found time to produce a voluminous outpouring of books and pamphlets (her *Notes on Nursing*

was an overnight success, with editions translated into Italian, German, French, and Czech), and to pursue an extensive international correspondence of over 13,000 letters, excerpts from which are quoted on the museum's wall panels.

But while Florence was often exceptionally compassionate toward the ill and the poor, the museum reveals how her relentlessness and self-righteousness could also intimidate the people closest to her, including the man who supported her unstintingly, Sidney Herbert. Disregarding his complaints of ill health as "fancies" (he had incurable kidney disease), she later confessed to a friend after his untimely death, "I, too, was hard on him."

Nonetheless, after a visit to this engrossing biographical museum, which does an outstanding job of introducing visitors to one of England's most intriguing and successful reformers, one cannot help but conclude that only a powerful personality such as Florence Nightingale could have brought such sanity to a brutal and bloody war, that only a formidable nature such as hers could have challenged the British Army, as well as a conservative medical establishment. After discovering this generous and comprehensive tribute to the life of a truly remarkable woman, one can only wish for more such marvelous mavericks.

FLORENCE NIGHTINGALE'S PARLOR
FURNISHINGS WERE TAKEN FROM HER
SOUTH STREET LONDON HOME,
WHERE SHE LIVED UNTIL HER DEATH
(AND WHICH HAS SINCE BEEN TORN DOWN).

Dennis Severs House

18 Folgate Street, Spitalfields
London E1 6BX
Tel: 0171–247–4013

Open on the first Monday of each month after twilight, and on the first Sunday of each month from 2:00 P.M. to 5:00 P.M. (Other special evening tours must be booked at least three weeks in advance.)

Underground: Take the Circle or Metropolitan Line to Liverpool Street Station.

THIS EARLY-EIGHTEENTH-CENTURY HOME IN SPITALFIELDS MAY BE THE ONLY HOUSE LEFT IN LONDON THAT IS LIT BY GASLIGHT; THE LAMP IS A BEACON TO GUESTS WHO HAVE COME TO DISCOVER THE DENNIS SEVERS HOUSE.

ON a quiet cobblestone street in Spitalfields, once renowned for producing some of the finest silks in the world, stands a handsome Georgian house built in 1724, whose bright red ground-floor shutters and flickering gas lamp pique the curiosity of the idle passerby. As the eye moves upward towards the second floor, the visitor cannot help but be struck by the silhouette of an elegant Georgian lady in one window, and that of a little boy playing with his pussycat in the other. On the top floor holding back the lace curtains is an older woman; is she real or is she merely painted onto the window? It is difficult to say.

Once inside the hall, you are immersed in the past, redolent with images recollected from films, books, and paintings. The door shuts, and suddenly you sense that you are not alone. A servant girl can be heard working upstairs, and you can hear the voices of several men in the dining parlor to your right. Outside in the street a change in the weather has brought out the street vendors, who are heard plying their trades. Someone on horseback rides by, as evidenced by the loud clip-clop of the horses. The delicious fragrance of roast beef and the smell of melting wax from the candles linger in the dining room, where the guests must have just finished their meal. Judging by the overflowing sideboard and the half-emptied goblets, the diners have fared well. The powdered wig of the master of the house has been removed and hangs from the finial of his chair. A clay pipe, which has just been smoked, rests on the table, next

THE REMAINS OF A TRADITIONAL ENGLISH BREAKFAST IN
THIS SPLENDID GEORGIAN BEDROOM—
LAVISHLY DECORATED WITH BLUE-AND-WHITE CHINA—
SUGGEST AN ELEGANT, LEISURED EXISTENCE.

to an enticing arrangement of fruit. Since the meal is over, the diners have left the room, leaving behind them the material evidence of their presence. The old brass clock ticks and tocks, the candles are still alight, the fire still smolders on the hearth, and the evocative sights, sounds, and smells overpower the intellect.

It is here, at the Dennis Severs House at 18 Folgate Street in London, that visitors are invited not merely to discover how people lived in the past, but to participate in what can best be called "a still-life drama," where guests are escorted into chambers from which, apparently, their eighteenth- and nineteenth-century inhabitants have only just withdrawn. Through the enthralling narrative at the Dennis Severs House, the visitor learns that this home once belonged to a family of master silk weavers of Huguenot descent, the Jervises. The rooms occupied by five generations of this unseen family present the leitmotifs that bound them to their own time: Enlightenment, Reason, Classicism, Romanticism, Reform, and later—in the nineteenth century —a return to practical Spirituality, embodied by the Victorian Age.

Severs guides his guests through the candlelit house, beginning in the dimly lit basement kitchen (inspired by illustrations in Beatrix Potter's *The Tailor of Gloucester*), where an inviting fire is burning in the grate and the large wooden table reveals the preparations of the kitchen scullery maid. The heavy, rustic sideboard is cluttered with painted crockery in all shapes and sizes; the rough pine table betrays the remains of breakfast. The room is filled with the smell of freshly-brewed coffee, scones, and buns. The visitors sit spellbound, drinking in every word Severs tells them about the Jervis family, be it about the ambitious Mrs. Jervis, who is determined to have her daughter marry well, or her household servant, who supplements her scant wages with petty thievery to buy herself a new ribbon for her bonnet.

Ever so obediently, the visitors trail their host up the narrow and time-worn stairs into a topsy-turvy smoking room the morning after a game of cards has taken place there. The chairs

THIS WRETCHED WORKROOM, WHICH ALSO DOUBLES AS LIVING QUARTERS, IS INTENDED TO REVEAL THE DECLINE IN FORTUNES OF THE SILK TRADE AT SPITALFIELDS, WITH ITS DIRE ECONOMIC CONSEQUENCES.

THE ROCK SUGAR CANDY, THE OVERTURNED CLAY PIPE, THE OVERFLOWING FRUIT BOWL,
AND THE POWDERED WIG ALL SUGGEST THE CONCLUSION OF DINNER
IN THE HOME OF A PROSPEROUS SILK MERCHANT IN GEORGIAN ENGLAND.

have been overturned, as have the glasses of wine on the table, and the room reeks of tobacco, sweet punch, and lemon rind. As the visitor's gaze turns to the painting above the mantel it becomes evident the picture is a reproduction of a painting by William Hogarth from *The Rake's Progress* that mirrors the contents and state of the room. The effect is carefully contrived: visitors are meant to

walk through a three-dimensional representation of an historical painting—in which every element is intended to serve Severs's "more interesting realities."

The visitors are then ushered into Mrs. Jervis's elegant Georgian drawing room, with its gilded swags of pinecones and nuts decorating the walls and its high-backed Georgian armchairs gravely facing one another.

THIS TEMPTING HALL CENTERPIECE LADEN WITH SWEETMEATS AND PETIT-FOURS PROVIDES AN INVITING DISPLAY AT THE FOOT OF THE DARK WOODEN STAIRCASE.

The room is set for tea, as shown by the delicate china cups laid out on the elegant mahogany tea-table before the fireplace. Suddenly, one is startled to hear the low murmuring of voices, the rustle of silk dresses, and a fan being dropped from one of the chairs. The inconceivable has occurred: bit by bit, room by room, the Jervises' household has come alive, to the point where the visitor seems to be sharing in their pastimes and pleasures—even being swept up in the historical and societal forces that informed and ultimately changed their existence.

In contrast to other museums in London that focus on faithfully re-creating the architecture and furnishings of a given period, the Dennis Severs House at Spitalfields attempts the impossible: inviting visitors to step into artfully imagined rooms that awaken all of their senses, exuding an unexpected drama and significance, thanks to Severs's compelling and erudite narrative. As you visit each room, you are invited to discover the daily life and habits of the Jervises, to learn how they became prosperous silk weavers, and how the family's fortunes altered with the decline of

Spitalfields. The house, unlike any other in London, is intended to be a palpable "document" of a family's triumph and tragedy, and attentive visitors will experience the curious sensation of participating in both—through an unexpected journey back in time.

"The game is, for you the visitor: the Jervises and their household have just walked off the stage as you enter. Thus you breathe the same air as they do. Everything you see is united by those you imagine," Severs explains with passionate conviction. "So, you will be amused, moved, stirred, delighted and—occasionally—saddened. You see their faces in the portraits; the very clothes worn two-dimensionally in these paintings are scattered about you in three. The ways in which chairs are positioned, tables laid, toys scattered, clay pipes and glasses put down for a moment, all beg your imagination to collude with them."

Whereas other historical houses in London are only intended for public viewing (and the odd special event), Severs has lived in his house since 1979, when he discovered it in near derelict condition. Contrary to other Londoners, he chooses to dwell in it, much as a family such as the Jervises might have lived down through the centuries, by candle and gaslight, using fires for cooking and for heat, even resorting to chamber pots. This deliberate, albeit unusual lifestyle, helps to create and strengthen the house's notable atmosphere.

However, Severs does not want visitors to imagine *him* in his own house. Instead, he has invented "an unseen third," the Jervises, as a mental device, to help visitors make sense of what they see. He insists that the only difference between the disorder created by domesticity and a still-life in his house is *"balance."*

THE HAUNTING SILHOUETTES IN THE WINDOWS REMIND VISITORS THIS HOUSE WAS ONCE PROBABLY OCCUPIED BY A FASHIONABLY DRESSED AND PROSPEROUS FAMILY.

Visitors, he maintains, will find this equilibrium all around them, holding their attention and asking for their respect.

With this kind of mission, it's not surprising that many curators and historians question such an approach to presenting the past. Is it a form of historical fiction? Is it theater? Is it a mystical vision of another reality? The host at 18 Folgate Street isn't saying. "It is the space between the eye and what you see that makes your visit here a rare experience. Don't allow that part of you held back by an 'average intelligence' to make you miss it. While you are here allow the House to persuade you with its poetry. The only art here, is *yours.*"

Sir John Soane's Museum

13 Lincoln's Inn Fields
London WC2
Tel: 0171–405–2107

**Open Tuesday through Saturday
10:00 A.M. to 5:00 P.M.
Also open the first Tuesday
of each month from 6:00 P.M.
to 9:00 P.M.**

**Underground: Take the Central
Line to Holborn Station.**

THE ENTRANCE TO THE MUSEUM
IS AT NO. 13 LINCOLN'S INN FIELDS,
THE MIDDLE HOUSE OF THREE
BUILT BY SIR JOHN SOANE.
HE BUILT NO. 12 IN 1792 (RECENTLY
RESTORED AND USED FOR
ADDITIONAL GALLERY SPACE),
NO. 13 IN 1812, AND NO. 14 IN 1824.
THE TOP STORY WAS ADDED
BY SOANE IN 1825.
THE TWO FIGURES OF COADE STONE
ON THE THIRD FLOOR
ARE INSPIRED BY CARYATIDS AT THE
ERECHTHEION IN ATHENS.

As a rule, London residences don't boast a sepulchral chamber containing an Egyptian sarcophagus, a closet full of Roman cinerary urns once used to store ashes of the dead, nor a human skeleton in an open cupboard. There is one exception however: 13 Lincoln's Inn Fields, the house and museum designed and lived in by Sir John Soane (1753–1837), England's pre-eminent Georgian architect, whose buildings include the Royal Hospital, Chelsea, the Dulwich Picture Gallery, and the Bank of England.

Soane, who was a compulsive collector (he even kept a case containing two mummified cats and a rat found while he was working on the Bank of England in 1803) lived, worked, and taught in this house for the last twenty-four years of his life. (Previously, he had lived next door in No. 12, which he had designed for himself in 1792, and which became part of the present museum in 1971.)

Deeply disappointed by the conduct of his two sons, John and George, neither of whom wanted to be architects, he decided to establish the house as a museum to which "amateurs and students" should have access, and to endow it with the bulk of his estate. (A contributing factor to Soane's decision was the publication of George Soane's anonymous article for *The Champion* reviling his father's architecture. The discovery of its authorship was described by Soane as "the death-blow" to his wife, who died that same year.)

Obtaining a private Act of Parliament (no small accomplishment) that placed the museum under a

THE RECENTLY RESTORED
BREAKFAST PARLOR AT NO. 12 LINCOLN'S INN FIELDS
(SOANE'S RESIDENCE FROM 1794 TO 1819)
IS BASED ON A PERIOD WATERCOLOR BY JOSEPH GANDY,
THE ARCHITECT'S FREELANCE PERSPECTIVE ARTIST.

board of trustees—a scheme that's in effect to this day—he stipulated that the House and Museum should be left virtually unchanged. Thanks to an outstanding team of curators and restorers, using Soane's own drawings and descriptions as their guide, his wishes have been largely respected.

It would be fair to say that there is no museum in the world that pays greater homage to the origins and evolution of Classical architecture. Soane's passion pervades every room, be it in the staggering amalgamation of antique architectural fragments, in the plaster and cork models of famous buildings and monuments (including one of Stonehenge), or

THE UPSTAIRS SOUTH DRAWING ROOM, REPAINTED ITS ORIGINAL "PATENT YELLOW,"
CONTAINS PORTRAITS OF SOANE AT AGE FIFTY-ONE AND OF HIS TWO SONS,
JOHN AND GEORGE, BY WILLIAM OWEN, FLANKING THE FIREPLACE.
THE WINDOW RECESSES WERE TRANSFORMED BY SOANE INTO BOOKCASES FOR
"GENERAL AND MISCELLANEOUS LITERATURE."

AMONG THE NOTEWORTHY EXHIBITS IN THE COMBINED DINING ROOM–LIBRARY,
ARE A PORTRAIT OF SIR JOHN SOANE BY SIR THOMAS LAWRENCE,
"ALMOST THE LAST PICTURE PAINTED BY THAT DISTINGUISHED ARTIST,"
AND A RARE APULIAN KRATER FROM THE LATE FOURTH CENTURY B.C.,
DISCOVERED AT LECCE IN 1790, AND LATER OWNED BY THE KING OF NAPLES.

in the collection of works on paper by the eighteenth century's two greatest draftsmen, the drawings of the Temples at Paestum by G.B. Piranesi (1720–1778) and the colored drawings of C.L. Clérisseau (1721–1821).

The museum is also a curious dichotomy of elegant simplicity and overwhelming clutter: whereas the two upstairs adjoining drawing rooms—the principal entertaining rooms of the house (repainted in Soane's original Patent Yellow)—are furnished sparely, the ground floor and basement are filled with what may seem an almost staggering accumulation of paintings, drawings, statuary, architectural fragments, vases, and medallions. To fully appreciate the museum's different facets, visitors are advised to take their time and to feel free to ask the well-informed staff to show them different highlights, some of which are not readily accessible, such as the Student's Room, where the architect's pupils drew from models.

As Soane's practice flourished—he became the first professor of architecture at the Royal Academy—his propensity to collect intensified, stimulated in part by the growing influx of ancient Greek and Roman antiquities available from London's leading auction houses. The collection reveals a man whose tastes were a reflection of the period in which he lived, and of an avant-garde aesthete who surpassed it. For instance, the same man who displayed works by his friend John Flaxman, such as the sculptor's models of the monuments for William Pitt and Lord Mansfield (the latter erected in Westminster Abbey), and a classical bust of himself by the sculptor Francis Chantrey, was also an early collector of stunning Peruvian pottery from the pre-Columbian period.

His acquisitions were frequently both magnificent and rare, such as an eight-day marine chronometer by the watchmaker Thomas Mudge (1717–1794), regarded as the finest copy in existence, and a cap badge of gold, set with rubies and diamonds (c. 1600), said to have come from the baggage of Charles I, captured after his defeat at the Battle of Naseby in 1645 during the English Civil War.

Soane's museum was also intended to reflect his own personal views on architecture, albeit with a touch of wry humor. Nowhere is this more evident than in the Monk's Parlour, a "Gothick" fantasy built around an imaginary monk, "Padre Giovanni," whose "tomb" and "cloister ruins" are visible through the window overlooking a courtyard, also known as the "cloister" or Monk's Yard. The Yard (hardly more than an airshaft) is composed of miscellaneous architectural fragments, consisting chiefly of fifteenth-century masonry from the Old Palace of Westminster, and an imposing marble tomb containing the remains of Fanny, a favorite dog.

With its brilliantly colored stained-glass window, Flemish wood carvings, dark polished wood furniture, and miscellaneous casts, most of which were taken from Medieval buildings and sculptures, the Parlour's atmosphere is one of intentional pretentious gloom, meant to "impress the spectator," says Soane, "with reverence for the monk." In fact, the message behind the Monk's Parlour is quite irreverent: "Padre Giovanni" is an eponym for John Soane, and the room's decor is meant to be an ironic comment on the fashionable cult of antiquarianism and the revival of Medieval Gothic—a style the architect vehemently opposed.

Connoisseurs of architecture will be delighted to discover that the house embodies many of Soane's finest experiments with light and space. While one could argue that the basement area exudes a certain gloom and mustiness—perhaps the appropriate atmosphere for the many antique architectural vestiges on display—the ground-floor and second-story rooms remain notable for their ingenious use of domed skylights and artfully placed mirrors, conveying a lightness and airiness notable for the period.

These effects are particularly evident in the two-story Dome (the oldest part of the present museum), with its colored glass skylights, and in the intimate Breakfast Parlour, whose shallow dome, pale yellow glass skylights, indirect lighting, and mirrors are Soanesian trademarks. It was in this latter room that he felt he had captured "the poetry of architecture."

Soane's space-saving display units and drawing cabinets are also worthy of study. The Picture Room, which was added to the house in 1824, is designed to accommodate enough pictures to fill a gallery more than three times its length. The architect was able to attain this seemingly

unrealistic goal only by hanging pictures right up to the ceiling (a common practice during the period) and by devising an elaborate system of hinged planes that open to reveal additional pictures inside. (Once again, Soane's sense of satire is evidenced in this room by the display of William Hogarth's two famous series of paintings, *The Rake's Progress* and *The Election.*)

In the North Drawing Room is the Dance Cabinet, designed by the architect to enclose the drawings of his teacher, George Dance (1741–1825), and a set of hidden swinging frames that pull out from the wall and contain Soane's drawings, as well as views of his own architectural designs.

For many visitors to this unique museum, the most extraordinary exhibit of all remains the nine-foot-long alabaster sarcophagus of the Egyptian Pharaoh Seti I (1301–1290 B.C.), discovered in his tomb chamber in the Valley of the Kings in 1817, by ex-circus strongman and amateur archaeologist G.B. Belzoni. When the British Museum declined to purchase it, Soane agreed to buy it for 2,000 pounds. The hieroglyphics, not interpreted until after Soane's death, constitute scenes and texts from *The Book of the Gates,* a religious work initiating worshipers of Osiris and Ra into the region through which their souls would pass after death.

To celebrate his acquisition, Soane hosted three separate evening receptions, one of which was attended by the poet Samuel Taylor Coleridge and the painter Joseph Mallord Turner. Another guest, Benjamin Robert Haydon, wrote to a friend about the occasion: "It was the finest fun imaginable to see the people come into the Library after wandering about below, amidst tombs and capitals, and shafts and noseless heads, with a sort of expression of delighted relief at

finding themselves among the living, and with coffee and cake. Fancy delicate ladies of fashion dipping their pretty heads into an old, mouldy, fusty hieroglyphicked coffin, blessing their stars at its age, wondering whom it contained."

Today, almost two centuries later, visitors to the Sir John Soane's Museum are still overcome with a sense of wonder—only now it is combined with an equal measure of admiration for the museum's founder, as well as for the accumulation of artwork and objects on display, whose power to fascinate and enthrall seems to defy the passage of time.

Spencer House

27 St. James Place
London, SW1
Tel: 0171–409–0526

**Open Sunday
February to July and September
to December for guided tours.
Tours every 15 minutes
10:45 A.M. to 4:45 P.M.
Phone 0171–499–8620 between
10:00 A.M. and 1:00 P.M. to
book a tour in advance.**

Disabled Access.

**Underground: Take the Piccadilly
Line to Piccadilly Circus.**

SPENCER HOUSE DEMONSTRATES
HOW TWO ARCHITECTS AND ONE LAVISH
PATRON CREATED ONE OF THE
MOST STUNNING EIGHTEENTH-CENTURY
MANSIONS IN LONDON.

OF the great London mansions built by the landed aristocracy during the eighteenth century, few are extant. With England's transition from an agrarian to an industrial economy, a significant decline in property values, compounded by the introduction of heavy death duties in the 1880s, meant that it was only a matter of time before the great residences in the heart of the city would become the target of developers and town planners. That is why the survival of Spencer House, one of London's last great town houses, built between 1756 and 1766 for the first Earl Spencer (an ancestor of the present Princess of Wales), is nothing short of miraculous.

Located in a quiet street in the heart of St. James's, a short distance from Buckingham Palace and the Palace of Westminster, Spencer House is viewed by connoisseurs not only as the first Neoclassical town house built in London, but as a milestone in the development of English taste. This splendid edifice, whose façade of white Portland stone stands out against the London skyline and the verdant expanse of Green Park, is a dazzling blend of the vision of two architects, John Vardy, a proponent of the Palladian style (whose inspiration came from the sixteenth-century Venetian Andrea Palladio), and James "Athenian" Stuart, an early champion of Neoclassicism and a pioneer of the Greek Revival. (Vardy was responsible for the building's exterior and the ground-floor apartments, while Stuart conceived the second-floor interiors, combining decoration and furniture that was directly inspired by the ancient world, particularly architectural remains from Greece and Rome.)

If visitors are able to appreciate the matchless splendors of Spencer House today, credit must go to both the seventh Earl Spencer (1872–1975), who resolutely hung on to the building between the wars, despite severe financial adversity, and to the present occupants, the James Rothschild group of companies, which—with the cooperation of the seventh Earl's descendants—has realized one of Great Britain's most ambitious and successful historic restorations.

Strolling through the lofty and splendidly decorated rooms, it is difficult to imagine that at the end of World War II, Spencer House was in total disrepair, with its façade

WHILE MUCH OF JOHN VARDY'S ORIGINAL DECORATION HAS BEEN LOST, THE REDECORATION OF THE WALLS, COVE CEILING, AND BALUSTRADE IS AN ACCURATE RE-CREATION OF THE ORIGINAL DESIGN.

blackened by smoke, its interiors stripped of ornament and furniture and piled high with rubbish, while yards of electric wiring dangled perilously from the ceilings. Although the house was hurriedly cleaned when Christie's, the auctioneers, became tenants in 1948, and kept up to a certain extent by subsequent tenants (which included the British Oxygen Company and *The Economist*), it was only returned to its former magnificence after an extremely lengthy and costly refurbishing program begun in 1985.

If Spencer House represents the epitome of Classical taste, it's not altogether surprising. The first Earl Spencer (1734–1783) was one of the eighteenth century's most extravagant

IN THE DINING ROOM, VARDY USED A NEOCLASSICAL FRIEZE OF SWAGS AND PUTTI
DERIVED FROM THE TEMPLE OF FORTUNA VIRILIS IN ROME.
THE ROOM'S GRANDEUR IS ENHANCED BY VARDY'S MAGNIFICENT PALLADIAN SIDE-TABLES,
ORNAMENTED WITH CARVED MASKS OF BACCHUS AND SUPPORTED BY WINGED PANTHERS.

and cultivated aristocrats (he spent a million pounds between the time he inherited the family fortune and his death). As an enthusiastic member of the Society of Dilettanti, whose aim was to revive English art and architecture through the promotion of Classical values, he encouraged and offered employment to designers of the burgeoning Neoclassical movement. Happily married to the exceptionally well-educated and musically talented Georgiana Poyntz, Spencer was keen to have a town house that would not only proclaim his wealth and status, but would also be a showplace for architecture and the decorative arts.

To accomplish this, he relied heavily on the judgment and expertise

IN THE PAINTED ROOM, JAMES "ATHENIAN" STUART MIXED MOTIFS FROM ANCIENT ROMAN AND RENAISSANCE WALL PAINTINGS WITH TOUCHES REMINISCENT OF GREEK SCULPTURAL ORNAMENT. THE SUITE OF FURNITURE HE DESIGNED FOR THIS ROOM COMPLETES THE OVERALL EFFECT OF DRAMATIC BRAVURA.

GEORGE JOHN, EARL SPENCER,
WHO WAS HAPPILY MARRIED TO THE
CULTIVATED AND MUSICAL GEORGIANA
POYNTZ, LIVED EXTRAVAGANTLY,
SPENDING 200,000 POUNDS THE YEAR
HE COMMISSIONED SPENCER HOUSE—
AN ENORMOUS SUM EVEN FOR HIS DAY.

of Colonel George Gray, the secretary of the Society of Dilettanti, a major figure in London's art world, who argued for archaeological accuracy in the reproduction of Classical elements. It was Gray who endorsed Vardy's appointment as the architect of Spencer House, only to have a hand in his dismissal later, by supporting a close friend, James Stuart, as Vardy's replacement.

Spencer House is the only London house with a monumental garden façade and a Classical temple front that conjures up visions of the Acropolis in Athens. Three stone deities preside over its pediment: Ceres, the goddess of corn and plenty; Flora, the goddess of flowers and gardens; and Bacchus, the god of wine and hospitality (also the mascot of the Society of Dilettanti). The austere entrance hall painted in

tones of gray and off-white, with stone flooring and a monumental inset plaster relief replica of the charioteer Antinous (cast after a celebrated Roman marble original excavated at Hadrian's Villa near Tivoli in 1735), demonstrates the eighteenth-century notion that such rooms were extensions of the exterior.

The forty-foot-long Great Eating Room, the largest of the ground-floor interiors and a sumptuous setting for large private dinners and public banquets, reflects the influence of the Palladian tradition. Its white-and-gold ceiling is derived from the one in the Banqueting House in Whitehall, conceived by the architect Inigo Jones; its pair of gilded wood sideboards (also a Vardy design), carved with masks of Bacchus and supported by winged panthers, pay homage to the Italian Renaissance. Still, not even the room's Neoclassical frieze of swags and putti, derived from the Temple of Fortuna Virilis in Rome, nor its impressive Ionic columns and pilasters prepare one for what comes next: the dazzlingly theatrical Palm Room, whose most conspicuous feature is a screen of Corinthian columns in the form of luxuriant palm trees. With its pea green walls, decorative plasterwork and joinery in white and gold, and alcove coffering rendered in a delicate shade of pink, it remains the most exotic Georgian interior in London.

However, not even such lavish decoration was enough to keep Vardy's patron happy. By 1758, it was decided that Spencer House required an architect more in tune with the Grecian taste and precepts then being espoused by the Society of Dilettanti. Gray advised the first Earl Spencer to commission James "Athenian" Stuart to design and decorate the rooms on the second floor, thus overruling designs already submitted by Vardy.

Initially, the commissioning of Stuart seemed a brilliant coup. Not only was he a leading architect, designer, and painter, he also was a distinguished scholar of Latin and Greek, as well as a noted archaeologist and author. His achievements were all the more remarkable considering he was born into poverty, had received little formal education, and spent a great part of his adult life in an acute state of inebriation. Despite the most promising and industrious start to his career, by the time he had obtained this splendid commission (it was to be his last), Stuart had begun a steady slide into dissipation and alcoholism. Had Spencer been aware of this, he might have hesitated to employ such an erratic talent.

Nonetheless, after eight years of delays and substantial cost-overruns, this patient patron did eventually see the completion of a stunning suite of Neoclassical rooms, regarded by many as Stuart's finest work. The most imposing of these is doubtless the Great Room, which was used for grand assemblies and balls. Its breathtaking coved ceiling, inspired by the Basilica of Maxentius in Rome and twice the height of any other room in the house, features coffered compartments painted in green, white, and gold and four bas-reliefs above the cornices, depicting figures from Classical mythology painted in imitation bronze, replicated from antique gems and medals.

Yet it is the adjoining brilliant green Painted Room (which takes its name from the murals and painted

IN DESIGNING THE ALCOVE IN THE ANTE-ROOM AT SPENCER HOUSE,
VARDY DREW HIS INSPIRATION FROM THE APSE IN THE TEMPLE OF VENUS AND ROME,
ILLUSTRATED IN ANDREA PALLADIO'S *QUATTRO LIBRI*.

inset panels that cover the walls and ceiling), that is generally viewed as the most consequential room at Spencer House, being the first fully integrated Neoclassical interior in England, and possibly in Europe. Although the room's murals and inset panels cover a wide range of subjects, the dominant theme is matrimony,

and this is clearly intended to celebrate the marriage of the first Earl and Lady Spencer. As in the Great Room, the sources of decoration are primarily Classical; the overall conception was taken from painted Roman interiors such as those that Stuart had seen on his tour of Pompeii and Herculaneum in 1748.

THE MANTELPIECE IN THE PAINTED ROOM IS A COMPOSITE OF DIVERSE ELEMENTS
DERIVED FROM GREEK, ROMAN, AND ITALIAN RENAISSANCE ART AND ARCHITECTURE,
AS WELL AS ECHOES OF SEVENTEENTH-CENTURY FLANDERS.

Although the delays in completing Spencer House fueled London's dinner-table conversation for years, in the end, visiting connoisseurs such as Arthur Young were astounded by the general conception and the splendor of its decorative scheme. "I do not apprehend there is a house in Europe of its size better worth the view of the curious in architecture and the fitting up and finishing of great houses than Lord Spencer's in St. James' Place," he observed in 1768. A tour of Spencer House today amply demonstrates that his informed opinion has brilliantly withstood the test of both taste and time.

Theatre Museum

National Museum of the
Performing Arts
Russell Street
Covent Garden
London WC2E 7PA
Tel: 0171–836–7891

**Open Tuesday through Sunday
11:00 A.M. to 7:00 P.M.
(Last admission at 6:30 P.M.)**

**Underground: Take the Piccadilly
Line to Covent Garden.
Bus: 6, 9, 11, 13, 15, 77A, 170,
176, 196**

THIS DISPLAY IS DEDICATED
TO MARIA TAGLIONI, THE FIRST ARTIST
TO WEAR WHAT BECAME
A CONVENTIONAL BALLET COSTUME
AND TO DANCE *EN POINTE*
TO EXPRESS CHARACTERS IN ROMANTIC
LITERATURE. AFTER HER PERFORMANCE
IN *LES SYLPHIDES*, SHE BECAME A
WORLD-FAMOUS BALLERINA,
WITH A REPUTATION THAT FEW HAVE
SINCE EQUALED.

I N 1576 Britain's first playhouse since Roman times—The Theatre —was built by the Earl of Leicester's Men. The timber-framed structure had three galleries roofed with thatch surrounding an open yard. Leicester's Men could perform anywhere in England, according to the Royal Patent of 1579, but wisely chose to build The Theatre in Finsbury Fields just outside the City of London, since the city fathers tended to frown upon play-going.

The first Bankside theater along the Thames was the Rose, which opened in 1587. William Shakespeare's first play, *Henry VI,* was staged there. Performances took place in daylight hours and the stage was a simple raised platform without curtains or set. All roles were played by men. Because there was no lighting and sound effects were few, all the drama had to emanate from the play's language. This lack of scenery and special effects didn't prevent the theater from becoming one of the most popular entertainments: within sixty years of the first theater's open-ing, no less than seventeen playhouses had sprung up around the City, the most famous among them being the Bear, the Rose, the Swan, and Shakespeare's Globe.

However, when the English Civil War broke out in 1642, barely twenty-six years after the Bard's death, Parliament closed all the theaters in London and made public performances of plays illegal. Anyone daring to defy the law could find his premises raided by soldiers, who ransacked buildings, imprisoned actors, and even fined audiences for

THIS STILL-LIFE OF PROGRAMS,
GREASEPAINT, CREAMS, PHOTOS, AND PLAYBILLS
CAPTURES THE THESPIAN MILIEU
IN AN EARLY TWENTIETH-CENTURY DRESSING ROOM.

attending this illicit form of entertainment. Playhouses would remain shut for an unprecedented eighteen years, until Charles II returned to the throne in 1660.

Fortunately, thespians and amateurs can now indulge their passion for theatrical history and memorabilia to their heart's content, as well as partake in makeup and costume workshops at the Theatre Museum (located in the heart of the stage district), which houses the world's most important collection of material pertaining to the British stage.

Visitors strolling through the museum's dimly lit lower level (where one can hear strains from such musicals as Andrew Lloyd Webber's *Phantom of the Opera*), will discover the costumes, playbills, props, and portraits of an array of major performing artists and entertainers who have graced the British stage for almost four hundred years: Nell Gwyn, who sold oranges in Covent Garden before becoming England's first celebrated comedienne (and mistress to Charles II); David Garrick, the first actor and director to champion Shakespeare, who banished spectators from the stage, initiated period dress, and made acting more naturalistic; Henry Irving, who dominated the English stage for twenty-five years and was the first actor to be knighted; or Maria Taglioni, the first ballerina to dance *en pointe* in *Les Sylphides.*

Even Queen Anne of Denmark was stagestruck: according to royal household accounts on display, Ben Jonson created a Queen's Masque that was staged at Whitehall Banqueting House in 1608 and cost 7,500 pounds to produce, a tidy sum considering that an artisan earned 15 pounds in a year. (A blend of theater and pageantry, these elaborate court masques, mainly designed by the architect Inigo Jones, were the first productions to use changeable scenery framed by a proscenium arch—long before the principle was adopted on the English public stage in the 1660s.)

The Theatre Museum is in a class by itself when it comes to presenting an overview of the evolution of

AMONG THE STAGE PROPS SHOWN HERE ARE A PAIR OF GLOVES WORN BY ACTOR HENRY IRVING WHEN HE PLAYED BENEDICK IN SHAKESPEARE'S *MUCH ADO ABOUT NOTHING,* A PROPERTY BOOK USED BY ELLEN TERRY IN HER ROLE AS PORTIA IN *THE MERCHANT OF VENICE,* AND A SKULL GIVEN TO SARAH BERNHARDT BY VICTOR HUGO FOR HER ROLE AS HAMLET.

THIS DISPLAY UNDERSCORES ONE OF THE
MOST SUCCESSFUL COLLABORATIONS IN THE BRITISH THEATER BETWEEN
W.S. GILBERT (1836–1911) AND ARTHUR SULLIVAN (1842–1900).
TOGETHER THEY WROTE FOURTEEN COMIC OPERAS—
INCLUDING *H.M.S. PINAFORE*, *THE PIRATES OF PENZANCE*, AND *THE MIKADO*—
IN WHICH SULLIVAN'S GENIUS AS A COMPOSER WAS MATCHED BY
GILBERT'S SKILL AS A PLAYWRIGHT AND HUMORIST.

different types of theatrical entertainment. The first theater built after the Restoration was Thomas Killigrew's Theatre Royal in Drury Lane, where Nell Gwyn performed. Royal support for the dramatic arts is illustrated by the Killigrew Patent, a 1662 ink and vellum document signed by Charles II granting exclusive monopoly of the London theater to Thomas Killigrew, who formed the King's Company. This document gave Killigrew and his heirs not only the right to assemble and manage a theatrical company, but in effect a virtual monopoly over the spoken drama. It would take nothing less than an Act of Parliament in 1843 to change this!

The King himself, a cultured man, encouraged innovations in staging that reflected Continental practices: actresses now replaced young male actors in female roles, and for the first time, plays were presented on the public stage with scenery. This led to building elaborate new playhouses that could accommodate changes in scenery and elaborate machinery, including cloud machines. Because the productions were costly and there was little financial security, it wouldn't be until 1675 that Thomas Betterton would break away to establish a second company in Lincoln's Inn Fields.

It was at John Rich's theater in Lincoln's Inn Fields that *The Beggar's Opera* by John Gay (which later inspired Bertolt Brecht's *The Threepenny Opera*), enjoyed sixty-three performances during its first season. The most popular work on the eighteenth-century stage—it was said to have made "Gay rich and Rich gay"—*The Beggar's Opera* (depicted in a fine William Blake engraving after a painting by William Hogarth) furthered the vogue for ballad opera featuring disreputable characters and dialogue mixed with lyrics set to well-known tunes.

Curtain time was much earlier during this period: one of the museum's oldest playbills advertising John Fletcher's *Rule a Wife and Have a Wife* in 1718, shows that the performance began at six o'clock in the evening. Actors, even then, were fairly well remunerated, being entitled to proceeds from a show, less basic house charges. A popular actress could earn as much as eighty pounds for a single performance, a substantial sum at the time.

It is thrilling to see an early draft of Richard Brinsley Sheridan's *The School for Scandal* with alterations written in his own hand. Although this was the most popular play during the remainder of the eighteenth century, Sheridan never produced a definitive version of it, nor did he sign his name to it.

Coming across the prompt script for the first production of George Bernard Shaw's *Saint Joan*, one is surprised to learn that this play was his first commercial success in over twenty years of playwriting. Many of G.B.S.'s early works were banned from public performance by the Lord Chamberlain, dealing as they did with such subjects as slum landlordism (*Widowers' Houses*), war and pacifism (*Arms and the Man*), and attacking the society that gave rise to such social ills.

Censorship is by no means the only travail that thespians have endured over the centuries. The museum's extensive displays on the development of theatrical makeup reveal just how perilous powder and paint could be. While rouge derived from the cochineal beetle was safe enough, ceruse, the most common makeup base in the nineteenth century, contained powdered white lead. It was highly toxic and a number of young beauties died from its usage.

Visitors today run no such risks in the demonstrations given by professional makeup artists at the Theatre Museum, as they learn that the boldness of makeup is often determined by the size of the theater and stage lighting. For instance, red foundation under a heavy matte base successfully camouflages the gray shadows of a beard and mustache and gives a smooth and velvety look to the skin.

While theatergoers often complain about the high price of tickets, it is difficult to imagine they would resort to rioting, as they did in London after

THIS RECONSTRUCTION OF AN EARLY PURPOSE-BUILT THEATER—SHAKESPEARE'S SECOND
GLOBE—SHOWS THAT THEATERS WERE STILL OPEN TO THE HEAVENS.
EARLY THEATERS WERE BUILT OUTSIDE THE CITY WALLS
TO AVOID THE JURISDICTION OF THE CITY FATHERS, WHO CONDEMNED PLAYS AS
"THE REST OF THE DEVIL AND THE SINK OF SIN."

Covent Garden's Theatre Royal raised the price of admission to boxes and the pit, and rented one tier of its boxes privately for the entire season, at a time when there were no reserved seats. The museum displays posters satirizing the theater's owners John Philip Kemble and Henry Harris, who miscalculated seriously in their decision to raise ticket prices to offset their building costs, and to provide funds for the engagement of popular Italian singers. The riots continued unabated for sixty-seven nights until mid-December 1809, when the proprietors finally capitulated and gave in to most of the rioters' demands.

Like all fine productions, the Theatre Museum is continuously renewing itself. Its latest venture is the establishment of a national video archive of stage performances that can be studied by scholars and thespians from all over the world. It already boasts a videotape library of over sixty-five live-recorded theatrical performances. It's nice to think of David Garrick at long last refuting his own mournful lines:

> But, he who struts his hour upon
> the stage,
> Can scarce extend his fame for
> half an age.

This highly entertaining and educational museum demonstrates just how long and with how much verve a theatrical performance can run.

Old St. Thomas's Operating Theatre, Museum, and Herb Garret

9A St. Thomas Street
London SE1 9RY
Tel: 0171–955–4791

Open Tuesday through Sunday
10:00 A.M. to 4:00 P.M.
Open Mondays for prebooked
groups.
(Closed except by special
appointment December 15 to
January 5.)

Underground: Take the Circle
Line to Monument, then walk
across London Bridge, down
a flight of stairs to St. Thomas
Street, and follow the signs
pointing to The Old Operating
Theatre.
Bus: 17, 21, 22A, 35, 40, 43,
44, 47, 48, 133, 501, 505, 510,
513, P3, P11

THIS GLEAMING KNIFE AND HACKSAW SET
WAS USED TO AMPUTATE THE LIMBS
OF UNFORTUNATE VICTORIAN PATIENTS
AT A TIME WHEN THERE WERE
NO ANESTHETICS. SPEED WAS THEN THE
SURGEON'S (AND THE PATIENT'S)
BEST HOPE; MANY OF THOSE OPERATED
ON DIED OF SHOCK, OTHERS
OF INFECTION.

"THE general arrangement of all the theatres was the same, a semi-circular floor and rows of semi-circular standings, rising above one another to the large skylight which lighted the theatre. On the floor the surgeon operating with his dressers, the surgeons and apprentices of both hospitals, and the visitors stood about the table, upon which the patient lay, and so placed that the best possible view of what was going on was given to all present. . . . The confusion and crushing was indeed at all times very great, especially when any operation of importance was to be performed, and I have often known even the floor so crowded that the surgeon could not operate till it had been partially cleared."

This account, given by John Flint South, surgeon to St. Thomas's Hospital from 1831 to 1863, brings vividly to life the pandemonium during surgery that was commonplace in the hospital's operating theater in the attic of St. Thomas's, an early eighteenth-century church near London Bridge and Southwark. Visitors who are willing to brave the flight of steep, narrow wooden steps leading to Old St. Thomas's Operating Theatre, Museum, and Herb Garret, can view the very room that South described, the only operating theater to survive from the days before the use of anesthetics and antiseptics. Imaginatively restored to underscore the contrast between modern surgery and the period before Dr. Joseph Lister (1827–1912) introduced antiseptic surgery, the theater remained hidden and largely forgotten until 1956, when its site within

THIS TABLEAU, WHICH SHOWS CHILD CARE TYPICAL IN LOCAL HOSPITALS
IN EDWARDIAN ENGLAND, IS BASED UPON THE ROYAL FAMILY'S VISIT IN JULY 1890
TO A WARD AT THE EVELINA HOSPITAL FOR SICK CHILDREN
ON SOUTHWARK BRIDGE ROAD, LONDON;
PRINCE EDWARD (LATER TO BECOME EDWARD VII) AND PRINCESS ALEXANDRA
ARE PORTRAYED NEXT TO BARON FERDINAND DE ROTHSCHILD,
THE FOUNDER OF THE HOSPITAL, AND ALICE CROSS, LADY SUPERINTENDENT.

the church's roof was identified by medical historian Raymond Russell. The theater and the herb garret are the only extant part of the original St. Thomas's Hospital, which was closed and moved to its present site in Lambeth in 1862.

Old St. Thomas's Hospital, one of London's oldest hospitals, is believed to have been founded in 1106 by Bishop Giffard of Winchester (around the same time as the priory of St. Mary Overie) and was in use until it burned in the fire at Southwark in 1212. Following the fire, it was rebuilt in 1215 to the east of Long Southwark (now Borough High Street), where the air was said to be sweeter. It was to remain on this site,

subject to a number of rebuilding programs, over the next 650 years. The present church was rebuilt by Thomas Cartwright, master mason to Sir Christopher Wren, between 1701 and 1703. (The original function of hospitals was to provide a place of general hospitality—hence the word's derivation—and it was only in the fourteenth century that they began to be used as centers for medical treatment.)

Surgical operations, however, could not be carried out by the religious staff. In 1163, the Council of Tours under Pope Alexander III had concluded that the shedding of blood was incompatible with the Holy Office. Surgery was therefore

THIS RECONSTRUCTED HERB GARRET IS MEANT TO CONVEY HOW THE ATTIC
WAS ONCE USED BY THE ST. THOMAS'S APOTHECARY TO STORE AND CURE HERBS
EARLY IN THE NINETEENTH CENTURY. THE USE OF THE GARRET
WAS CONFIRMED BY THE DISCOVERY OF FOUR POPPIES, HOOKS, EYES, NAILS, ROPES,
AND OTHER DEVICES FOR HANGING HERBS FROM RAFTERS.

relegated to barbers, and regarded throughout the Middle Ages as a secular, low-status profession, which it remained until the nineteenth century.

When it was built in 1821, the Operating Theatre was used exclusively for operations on poor women (the affluent were operated on in the comfort of their own homes), which at the time were performed in appallingly unhygienic conditions. The struggling patients, who were often held down by several assistants (in the days before anesthesia), not only tolerated an audience to their distress, but submitted to amputation, bleeding, and even trepanning, which consisted of boring holes in the patient's skull. (It wasn't until 1846 that the theater witnessed the use of anesthesia.)

Seeing the arena-like room's yellow ocher walls (the original color), crude wooden operating table, wooden washstand with a small blue-and-white china basin and ewer, and antiquated surgical instruments laid out on green baize, it is hard to believe this operating theater, in its heyday, was regarded as one of the most modern in London.

The concept of an operating theater being pristine and free of sepsis is a relatively recent innovation. Similarly, aseptic furniture made of steel and glass was not introduced until the 1880s. Surgeons operated in black frock coats and tended to wash their hands and instruments *after* rather than before or between operations—a major cause of fatal

THE DRIED HERBS ON DISPLAY IN THE GARRET
WERE CHOSEN BASED ON EIGHTEENTH-CENTURY LEDGERS
KEPT BY APOTHECARIES AT GUY'S AND ST. THOMAS'S HOSPITALS:
THYME, POPPIES, ROSEMARY, MUSTARD SEED, WORMWOOD,
AND RHUBARB ALL FIGURED ON THEIR LISTS.

post-operative infections. Needless to say, the wearing of surgical gloves was not even contemplated.

The appalling conditions of the era's operating theaters are confirmed by J.R. Leeson, who was house-surgeon to Lister in 1872: "There were no basins for washing hands, such matters were not considered; in the centre of the worn and blood-stained floor, sprinkled with sawdust, was the operating table, an ordinary kitchen table devoid of any acces-sories. . . . The operating table looked as if it was never washed. . . . There was no removal of coats and only an occasional turning up of sleeves; everything was ordinarily dirty, and for our modern standpoint unthink-able." (It wasn't until the 1890s that surgical white overalls and antiseptic

treatment were widely adopted in London.)

Not only was surgery a patient's last resort, it tended to be limited to amputations, strangulated hernias, the removal of cataracts, easily accessible skin cancers, as well as kidney stones—operations which, while unpleasant, were usually not lethal. The absence of anesthesia meant that speed was essential: one surgeon from Guy's Hospital was cited for amputat-ing a leg in twenty-seven seconds!

The museum's impressive display of surgical instruments that were in use in the mid-nineteenth century, reveals how they differed little from those used in Roman times. Trepanning, which goes back to prehistoric times (when it was believed that drilling a hole in a sick

IN 1822, THE AUTHORITIES AT ST. THOMAS'S HOSPITAL CONVERTED PART OF THE ROOF SPACE OF THE CHURCH INTO AN OPERATING THEATER FOR THE ADJACENT WOMEN'S WARD SO THAT THE VICTIMS' SCREAMS WOULD NOT DISTURB THE PATIENTS IN THE WARDS. HERE, WITHOUT THE BENEFIT OF ANESTHETICS OR ANTISEPTIC PROCEDURES, SURGEONS PERFORMED OPERATIONS (FREE OF CHARGE) IN FRONT OF AUDIENCES COMPOSED OF MEDICAL STUDENTS. ONE NINETEENTH-CENTURY STUDENT CONFESSED: "THE MORE THE PATIENT DID CRY OUT, THE MORE WE DID LAUGH."

person's head would release evil spirits), was still one of the most widespread operations during this period.

Adjacent to the operating theater is the museum's fragrant herb garret, once used for the storage and curing of medicinal herbs, which dates back to the church's construction. The use of herbs in the hospital was first recorded during the Elizabethan period. In 1605, it was reported that a medicinal bath for a woman in the Judith Ward at St. Thomas's was prepared with the use of herbs and sheep heads. A century later, one of the hospital's physicians, Dr. Richard Mead, was recommending a cure for venereal diseases that contained such ingredients as crushed garden snails, wormwood, ground ivy, juniper berries, fennel seeds, anise, and cloves—all of which were mixed with wine and springwater.

To convey an atmosphere of authenticity, many of the herbs that were supplied to apothecaries in the 1830s, including ropes of garlic (to cure the common cold), marshmallow (an herb used to help digestion), and willow bark (it contains salicin, an ingredient in aspirin), are suspended from the garret's wooden beams. The Georgian apothecary counter displays not only an impressive array of herbs in baskets, but also some of the types of mortars, pestles, and metal bell jars that the apothecary's assistant would use to pound and grind herbal remedies.

To some delicate constitutions, the history of Old St. Thomas's Operating Theatre, Museum, and Herb Garret might seem as hard to ingest as one of Dr. Mead's potions.

Yet even the most squeamish visitors can value this atypical museum, which does a highly commendable job of shedding light on a time that was a turning point in surgery, and which helps one to appreciate (and be thankful for) just how far medicine has progressed.

THIS NINETEENTH-CENTURY WOODEN OPERATING TABLE IS VERY LOW BY MODERN STANDARDS, BEING ONLY SIXTY CENTIMETERS HIGH. DURING OPERATIONS THE TABLE WAS COVERED WITH A BLANKET OVER WHICH WAS THROWN A LARGE SHEET OF BROWN OILCLOTH.

Waddesdon Manor

**The Rothschild Collection
Near Aylesbury
Buckinghamshire HP18 OJH
Tel: 1296–651282**

**House open Thursday through
Saturday from 12:30 P.M. to
6:00 P.M.; Sunday from 11:00 A.M.
to 6:30 P.M., March 28 to
October 13. (House also open
Wednesday during July and
August.) Grounds, aviary, shop
and restaurant open Wednesday
through Sunday from 11:00 A.M.
to 5:00 P.M.**

- **By train: Monday through
Saturday, take the Bakerloo Line
to Marylebone Station, then
take train to Aylesbury. From
Aylesbury, take a ten-minute taxi
ride to the Manor. On Sunday,
take the Metropolitan Line to
Baker Street Station to Amersham
Station, then take train to
Aylesbury.**
- **By car: From Junction 16 of the
M25 ring road to the west of
London, take the M40 in the
direction of Oxford. Leave the
M40 either at Junction 7 towards
Thame/Aylesbury or at Junction 9
towards Bicester. Waddesdon
village is on the A41 road between
Aylesbury and Bicester, and the
entrance to the Manor is well
indicated.**

Restaurant on premises.

"THAT the Sovereign of this realm who, for the last thirty years, has lived in almost complete privacy, should have found my house an attraction so exceptional as to draw her from seclusion, was highly gratifying to myself; but that gratification was enhanced by the fact that the Queen, as I have been informed by the Prince of Wales and every member of her household I have seen, was thoroughly delighted with the arrangements I had made for her comfort, and with the place itself."

So wrote Baron Ferdinand de Rothschild, recollecting the visit of Queen Victoria to Waddesdon Manor in Buckinghamshire in 1897 (seven years after the event). He had every reason to exult over the success of her sojourn there, which had taken over eighteen months to organize. Victoria was so captivated by the interior decoration, furnishings, and room arrangements at the Rothschild country house that, following her visit, she sent the superintendent of Windsor Castle to inspect them. Equally impressed by the excellence of the Baron's table, she not only took away three copies of the luncheon menu that was served, but subsequently sent the Royal Cook to take lessons from the Manor's cook.

More than a century later, a tour of the splendidly restored country house in the rolling green hills of Buckinghamshire provides ample evidence as to why even the world's most powerful and influential queen might desire to emulate her host's taste and hospitality. Every element is conceived to enchant and enthrall, whether it's the sight of a group of

THE ROUNDABOUT OF THE NORTH FOUNTAIN OFFERS
A FRONTAL VIEW OF WADDESDON MANOR.
IN ITS CENTER IS THE EIGHTEENTH-CENTURY FOUNTAIN OF *TRITON AND NEREIDS*
BY G. MOZANI, WHICH—TOGETHER WITH SOME FIGURES
FROM THE ESTATE'S SOUTH FOUNTAIN—
ONCE STOOD IN THE GARDEN OF THE DUCAL PALACE OF COLORNO,
NEAR PARMA, ITALY.

snow-white monkjack deer resting under the estate's splendid trees, a brilliant profusion of plantings in the late-Victorian formal garden, exquisite examples of eighteenth-century tapestries, *boiseries*, and furniture (many of which were once owned by the French royal family and aristocracy), or the stunning group of seventeenth-century Dutch masters and eighteenth-century English portraits by Reynolds, Gainsborough, and Romney. Strolling through the twenty-seven beautifully appointed rooms open to the public, which despite their grand scale manage to convey an unexpected intimacy, one can understand why the Baron's weekend house parties drew such luminaries as the Prince of Wales, Henry James, Guy de Maupassant, and the Shah of Persia.

Baron Ferdinand de Rothschild (1839–1898), the great-grandson of Mayer Amschel (1744–1812), founder of the greatest European banking dynasty, built Waddesdon Manor between 1874 and 1889, after purchasing the vast estate from the Duke of Marlborough. Designed by the architect Gabriel-Hippolyte Destailleur in the style of the French Renaissance, this Bath-stone country house of over two hundred rooms could easily be compared to a château in the Loire Valley. Although Baron Ferdinand had chosen to make his home and political career in England

WHEN BARON FERDINAND DE ROTHSCHILD BUILT WADDESDON MANOR, HE WAS INSPIRED BY THE
CHÂTEAUX OF THE VALOIS IN TOURAINE, FRANCE. THE SOUTH TERRACE AND PARTERRE
EPITOMIZE THE LATE VICTORIAN TASTE FOR A MASSIVE DISPLAY OF BOLD COLOR; KNOWN AS
"RAISED RIBBON BEDDING," THE TECHNIQUE CONSISTS OF MOUNDING THE CENTER OF THE
FLOWER BED AND FRAMING IT WITH TIERED BORDERS, THUS CREATING "RIBBONS" OF COLOR.

(he was a Liberal Member of Parliament for Aylesbury from 1885 until his death fourteen years later), when it came to architecture and the decorative arts, his heart and soul belonged to France. While he didn't have the purse of a French king, he was nonetheless keen to build a home that was inspired by the most outstanding châteaux, a predilection he made clear in his memoirs. "By the side of the grand châteaux of the Touraine, Waddesdon would appear a pygmy. . . . But its main features are borrowed from them; its towers from Maintenon, the château of the Duc de Noailles, and its external staircase from Blois. . . . Though far from being the realization of a dream in stone and mortar like Chenonceaux, M. Destailleur's work had fairly fulfilled my expectations."

THE DINING-ROOM TABLE IS DECORATED AS SHOWN IN A PHOTOGRAPH TAKEN IN 1897.
ALL THE PORCELAIN IN THE ROOM WAS MADE AT THE GERMAN MEISSEN FACTORY
DURING THE EIGHTEENTH CENTURY.
THE TWO BEAUVAIS TAPESTRIES COME FROM A SERIES TITLED *LA NOBLE PASTORALE*,
DESIGNED BY FRANÇOIS BOUCHER AND WOVEN BETWEEN 1755 AND 1778.

Knowing the herculean efforts that it took to transform the estate's wilderness into a park, to build roads on the property, to level the hilltop for the house and the north lawns, to provide adequate foundations, and even to create a special railway to bring the Bath stone and building bricks to the hill's base, the Baron's summation seems an understatement. Period photographs reveal how a small army of workers was employed to dig, level, drain, and build, assisted by a team of Percheron mares imported from Normandy, which carted the Bath stone and the large trees from the surrounding area—the same trees then being transplanted on the estate. This vast undertaking often proved so daunting to the Baron that, during the first four years of construction, he rarely went near the site. It wasn't until 1880 that he first slept in the "bachelor's wing," and in 1883, in the main part of the house.

Inside the house, the visitor sees the combined collections of Baron Ferdinand, his younger sister Alice, and James de Rothschild (whose contribution came to him by inheritance from his father, Baron Edmond, in 1934). However, the style of the house was established by Baron Ferdinand, whose purchases throughout his life were guided by his knowledge of French decorative arts and his exceptional eye for quality. His intention was to furnish the house with the greatest elegance and comfort—"reconstructing rooms out of old material, reproducing them as they had been during the reigns of the Louis." The eighteenth-century carved oak paneling taken from elegant Parisian mansions, which were being pulled down to make way for new streets during the Second Empire, provides a stunning backdrop for the myriad paintings and furnish-

THE IMPOSING BLACK LACQUER
SECRÉTAIRE IN THE MORNING ROOM,
ALTHOUGH MADE BY
TWO FRENCH CRAFTSMEN, RENÉ DUBOIS
AND JACQUES GOYER,
WAS PROBABLY COMMISSIONED
BY A PATRON OUTSIDE FRANCE
WHO REMAINS UNIDENTIFIED.
THE BRONZE EAGLE HOLDS EMBLEMS
OF PEACE AND WAR,
WHILE THE FIGURES REPRESENT
FORCE AND MAGNANIMITY.

ings, and forms a unique assemblage found nowhere else outside of France.

Waddesdon has at least twelve pieces of furniture made for the French royal family by leading Parisian cabinetmakers, including a pair of chest of drawers by Jean-Henri Riesener, one of which was ordered in 1776 for the bedroom in Versailles of Louis XVI's sister-in-law, the Comtesse de Provence, and the other in 1778, for the King's sister, Madame Elisabeth, when she was fourteen years old.

The most distinctive piece of furniture is without a doubt the massive cylinder-top desk made by an unknown cabinetmaker in 1779 and given to P.-A. Caron de Beaumarchais by his friends. Beaumarchais, best

THE MORNING ROOM, WHERE GUESTS COULD ATTEND TO THEIR CORRESPONDENCE
AND READ, WAS BUILT IN 1889, NEARLY A DECADE AFTER THE REST OF THE HOUSE.
BESIDES BOASTING A FINE COLLECTION OF DUTCH, FLEMISH, AND ENGLISH PAINTINGS,
IT CONTAINS SOME OF THE BEST FRENCH FURNITURE IN THE HOUSE,
AS WELL AS FOUR SAVONNERIE CARPETS. THE PAINTING ABOVE THE FIREPLACE IS JOSHUA
REYNOLDS' PORTRAIT OF EMILY POTT AS *THAIS*, THE ATHENIAN COURTESAN WHO URGED
ALEXANDER THE GREAT TO BURN THE ROYAL PALACE OF PERSEPOLIS.

remembered as the author of *The Marriage of Figaro* and *The Barber of Seville,* was a sympathizer with the aims of the American Revolution and a secret political agent for Louis XVI. The titles of two of his political pamphlets are worked into the marquetry of the desk's writing flap; the first, written in 1776, urged that France should recognize the independence of the United States, and the other, penned in 1779, is a reply to an attack by Edward Gibbon (author of *The Decline and Fall of the Roman Empire*), charging France with secretly supplying arms to the rebellious British colonies. The desk was sold by lottery in Paris during the July Revolution of 1830; one of the fifty-

franc lottery tickets is preserved in a frame on the side of the desk.

While Waddesdon Manor presents a superb collection of paintings, furniture, and decorative arts, it also provides visitors with an opportunity to learn more about the history of a remarkable family that has made its mark in the worlds of finance and politics. In the recently refurbished family rooms on the second floor, one learns how the second Lord Rothschild, Lionel Walter (1868–1937), was a fervent supporter of the Zionist desire to establish a national homeland for Jews in Palestine. His successful lobbying of the British government resulted in the Balfour Declaration, a letter written to him by Lord Balfour, the Foreign Secretary in 1917, confirming the British government's intention to facilitate the attainment of this objective.

A year before his death at the age of fifty-nine, Baron Ferdinand expressed his concern about Waddesdon Manor: "A future generation may reap the chief benefit of a work which to me has been a labor of love, though I fear Waddesdon will share the same fate of most properties whose owners have no descendants, and fall into decay. May the day yet be distant when weeds will spread over the garden, the terraces crumble into dust, the pictures and cabinets cross the Channel or the Atlantic, and the melancholy cry of the nightjar sound from the deserted towers." After a visit to this incomparable country estate, it seems ever so clear that the Baron's fervent hope is being fulfilled every day at Waddesdon Manor.

THE WADDESDON AVIARY, BUILT BY BARON FERDINAND DE ROTHSCHILD, IS A RARE EXAMPLE OF A WORKING AVIARY HOUSED INSIDE A HISTORICAL STRUCTURE. THE RECENTLY RESTORED BUILDING IS STOCKED WITH A VARIETY OF COLORFUL BIRDS, INCLUDING A DAZZLING FAIRY BLUEBIRD, A PEACH-FACED LOVEBIRD, AND AN EMERALD STARLING.

**Hertford House
Manchester Square
London W1M 6BN
Tel: 0171–935–0687**

Disabled Access.

**Open Monday through Saturday
10:00 A.M. to 5:00 P.M.;
Sunday 2:00 P.M. to 5:00 P.M.**

**Underground: Take the Central
or Jubilee Line to Bond Street;
the Wallace Collection is a
five-minute walk from the tube
station and Oxford Street.
Bus: (Stopping at Selfridges,
a five-minute walk from the
Wallace Collection), 2, 6, 7, 10,
12, 13, 15, 16A, 23, 30, 73,
74, 82, 94, 98, 113, 135, 137,
139, 159.**

"THERE is nothing else in London like the Wallace Collection; it is a little Louvre Museum. There is probably in the world no more surprising display of the acquisitive abilities of a few wealthy and cultivated aristocrats. It is also the most splendid gift ever made to the nation by an individual."

The unabashed admiration and awe expressed by H.V. Morton in his book *In Search of London* are sure to be shared by any visitor who has the good fortune to visit Hertford House, one of the most impressive small museums in the world, which remains, nonetheless, one of the city's best-kept secrets, despite wide acclaim by aesthetes and scholars.

"The Wallace Collection's greatest strength is its extraordinary array of French eighteenth-century decorative arts and paintings: Sèvres porcelain, furniture and snuffboxes of the highest quality, often acquired from royal collections, displayed together with exquisite and sensuous works by Boucher, Watteau, and Fragonard," notes director Rosalind Savill. "As if this were not enough, the museum also boasts masterpieces by Titian, Poussin, Rembrandt, Rubens, Velázquez, and Hals, the finest collection of arms and armor in England outside the Tower of London, as well as exceptional Medieval, Renaissance, and Baroque works of art, including

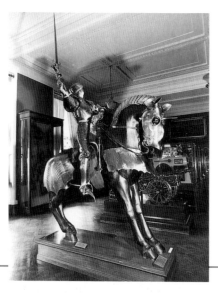

THE ELEGANT FORM AND SHELL-LIKE FLUTING OF THIS GOTHIC WAR HARNESS FOR MAN AND HORSE IS CHARACTERISTIC OF GERMAN FIFTEENTH-CENTURY ARMOR AT ITS BEST. IT WAS PROBABLY MADE FOR A MEMBER OF THE BAVARIAN FREYBURG FAMILY.

HERTFORD HOUSE, WHICH WAS DESIGNED BY JOSHUA BROWN, WAS BUILT
AS MANCHESTER HOUSE IN 1766–88 FOR THE FOURTH DUKE OF MANCHESTER.
AFTER A BRIEF SPELL AS THE SPANISH EMBASSY,
IT WAS LEASED TO THE SECOND MARQUESS OF HERTFORD, WHO WAS ATTRACTED BY
THE GOOD DUCK SHOOTING IN THE AREA.
IN 1872, SIR RICHARD WALLACE COMMISSIONED THE ARCHITECT
THOMAS AMBLER TO UNDERTAKE A VAST PROGRAM OF ALTERATIONS THAT INCLUDED
INSTALLING A MINTON-TILED SMOKING ROOM ON THE GROUND FLOOR AND
SKYLIGHTED GALLERIES ON THE SECOND.
AFTER WALLACE'S DEATH, THE ENTIRE HOUSE WAS CONVERTED INTO A MUSEUM.

jewelry, glass, majolica, painted enamels, wax miniatures, and illuminated manuscripts."

The works of art that make up this remarkable collection were largely assembled by one man: the fourth Marquess of Hertford. His forbears, particularly the third Marquess, also contributed significantly, as did his illegitimate son and heir, Sir Richard Wallace. It was in Wallace's honor that his widow bequeathed the collection to the nation with the stipulation that it "shall be kept together, unmixed with other objects of art."

The museum's sumptuously decorated rooms boast the finest collection of Sèvres porcelain in the world, including six pieces from the service of Russia's Empress Catherine the Great, commissioned in 1776 and delivered to the Hermitage in St. Petersburg in 1779. Numbering 797 pieces in total, this Neoclassical service with its turquoise blue (*bleu céleste*) ground and cameo heads, was destined to become one of the most expensive services ever produced in Europe. The plates alone were redesigned eight times and over 3,000 pieces were made to ensure that the 800 needed would meet the Empress's exacting standards. In 1837, over one hundred pieces were looted after a fire at the Hermitage, and found their way to London, where they were eventually acquired by the fourth Marquess. However, after deciding to retain six of the most elaborate pieces for himself (the wine and ice-cream coolers), he sold

THE MOST STRIKING FEATURE OF THE FRONT ENTRANCE HALL
IS THE STAIRCASE AND BALUSTRADE.
THE BALUSTRADE WAS ORIGINALLY PART OF THE
FRONT STAIRCASE IN THE FORMER HÔTEL DE NEVERS IN PARIS,
WHICH UNDER SCOTTISH FINANCIER JOHN LAW
HOUSED THE *BANQUE ROYALE*.

the rest back to Tsar Alexander II (reigned 1855–1881).

Just as outstanding is the museum's collection of Boulle marquetry furniture, assembled over a period of fifty years, and which at one time enjoyed great favor at the French Court. Named after André-Charles Boulle (1642–1732), its fabrication combines tortoiseshell (actually obtained from the shells of sea turtles) and brass; the two materials are cut out together by a craftsman using a marquetry saw, then glued onto the oak or pinewood surface of the furniture.

The family that amassed this unique and unequaled collection turns out to be as remarkable as the museum itself. The first family member to take a serious interest in collecting was Francis Charles Seymour-Conway, third Marquess of Hertford (1777–1842), who increased his family's wealth by marrying Maria Fagnani, the illegitimate daughter of a former dancer. Maria enjoyed an unusual financial advantage: two extremely rich men, the fourth Duke of Queensberry (known as "Old Q," whose portrait by Joshua Reynolds hangs at Hertford House) and his associate George Selwyn, both believed they were her father. When they died, they both left her substantial fortunes.

Two years after the fourth Marquess was born, his parents

separated. In fact, the third Marquess led a life of such epic self-indulgence that he inspired unsavory characters in novels by William Makepeace Thackeray and Benjamin Disraeli. Still, not all of his wealth went to waste: like his friend, the Prince of Wales, later George IV (who was infatuated with the third Marquess's mother), he favored seventeenth-century Dutch paintings displayed with opulent Boulle furniture, gilt bronzes, and Sèvres porcelain. To the Wallace Collection he brought some exceptional bronzes, thirty pieces of Sèvres porcelain, and one of Titian's most important works, *Perseus and Andromeda*, painted for Philip II of Spain and later owned by the painter Anthony van Dyck.

This painting now hangs in the Main Gallery, the largest room at Hertford House, which offers one of the finest presentations of seventeenth-century European painting to be seen anywhere in the world, most of which were acquired by the fourth Marquess. Among the prize works on view are Nicolas Poussin's allegorical *A Dance to the Music of Time*, Rembrandt van Rijn's moving portrait of his son *Titus* at the age of sixteen (painted shortly after the artist's bankruptcy), Peter Paul Rubens's *The Rainbow Landscape* (a celebration of the Brabant countryside, it was painted after the artist retired), and Frans Hals's world-renowned *Laughing Cavalier*.

With such an accumulation of choice works, it is no wonder that Richard Seymour-Conway, fourth Marquess of Hertford (1800–1870) has been acclaimed as the greatest private collector of the nineteenth century. Brought up in Paris by his mother, he felt himself as much French as English, and vastly preferred his Parisian residences to Hertford House. Never married, the witty and intelligent Marquess was one of the richest men in Europe and an intimate of Napoleon III. Like his father, he was attracted to the superb craftsmanship of the Ancien Régime, although he acquired a much wider range of objects (many of which he never set eyes upon). In addition to Flemish and Dutch masterpieces, he collected contemporary painting by Horace Vernet, Eugène Delacroix, and Richard Parkes Bonington, eighteenth-century French works ranging from Watteau to Greuze, as well as miniatures, gold boxes, tapestries, and sculpture from the same period and—later in life—Oriental arms and armor.

"The fourth Marquess inherited his father's intelligence but not his sociability, preferring to live a reclusive life centered around his beloved collection," notes Savill. "Notoriously mean, like many rich men, he could be witty and charming when it suited him. He never married, although he cruelly deceived one of his mistresses, Madame Oger, by arranging a mock marriage ceremony in which his valet was dressed as a clergyman."

That wasn't the only deception he practiced upon the people closest to him. When he died in 1870, he left nearly all his property to his son Richard Wallace (1818–1890), who had been his secretary and adviser. Yet it was only after his father's death that Wallace (who had taken his mother's maiden name) learned that the fourth Marquess was his father.

In 1870–71, when Paris was devastated by the Communard uprising, Wallace gave huge sums of money to charity, as well as most famously, fifty public drinking fountains, known to this day in Paris as *wallaces* (one is in the museum's front garden). It was for his charitable work on behalf of the British community in Paris that he was awarded a baronetcy in 1871. That same year he also married his

THE LARGEST ROOM IN HERTFORD HOUSE, THE GRAND PICTURE GALLERY,
SHOWS ONE OF THE FINEST COLLECTIONS OF EUROPEAN PAINTING
TO BE SEEN ANYWHERE IN THE WORLD, WITH WORKS BY TITIAN, PHILIPPE DE CHAMPAIGNE,
NICOLAS POUSSIN, AND SALVATORE ROSA.

mistress, Amélie-Julie Castelnau (1819–1897), the mother of his thirty-year-old son, Edmond Richard. However, this was not a marriage of social equals brought together by mutual interests: the cigar-smoking Lady Wallace had been a perfume-seller when she met her future husband, and there is no evidence that she shared his enthusiasm for art collecting.

Troubled by the political situation in France, Wallace moved back to London in 1872 with his wife and son, and settled in Hertford House, bringing many of his finest works of art with him. Following the death of his son in 1887, he returned alone to the Château de Bagatelle where he died in 1890, in the same room as had his father.

In reflecting upon the fact that a single family was able to acquire so many works of art of such exquisite quality, one may wonder, as did H.V. Morton, "whether the possession of so many superb things brought happiness with it, and if so, was such happiness due to the objects themselves or the sense of possession, which can be a powerful emotion almost akin to love, pity and hate." While such a conundrum may never be answered, now that the Wallace Collection is no longer a jealously guarded private domain, its dazzling accumulation of treasures can be fully and freely admired by all who find their way to Hertford House.

Wimbledon Lawn Tennis Museum

**All England Club
Church Road
Wimbledon SW19
Tel: 0181–946–6131**

**Open Tuesday through Saturday
10:30 A.M. to 5:00 P.M.;
Sunday 2:00 P.M. to 5:00 P.M.**

- **Underground: Take the District
  Line to Southfields. (The museum
  is a fifteen-minute walk from the
  station.)**
- **By bus: 39, 93, and 200**
- **By train: Take the train from
  Waterloo Station to Wimbledon.
  (The museum is a short cab ride
  from the station.)**

Tearoom.

CENTRE COURT,
WHICH CAN BE SEEN DURING
A VISIT TO THE
WIMBLEDON LAWN TENNIS MUSEUM,
CAUSED TENNIS CHAMPION
PETE SAMPRAS TO OBSERVE:
"YOU CAN FEEL THE HISTORY THERE.
CENTRE COURT IS THE
ONE COURT EVERY PLAYER WISHES
HE COULD PLAY ON."

FEW people realize that the heart-stopping game they watch at Wimbledon, lawn tennis, is a direct descendant of a medieval game known as Real, Royal, or Court Tennis, first played in France in the twelfth century by bishops and priests in cloisters. The game was then called *jeu de paume*, because the ball was hit with the palm of the hand. Later, the hand was protected by a special glove, which eventually was supplanted by a short, simple, paddle-like racket. However, it wasn't until the sixteenth century that the powerful racket used in Real Tennis came into being, with its longer handle, distinctively curved head, and strong gut strings. By then, Real Tennis had become a royal and popular game, played throughout Europe by kings and their courtiers at their castles and palaces.

It would take the Industrial Revolution to transform Real Tennis into a game for the upper-middle classes, who now had the leisure, energy, and means to participate in sports. However, they wanted a simpler game that could be played in the open air and by men and women together. Lawn tennis seemed to be the answer. Yet without two critical nineteenth-century inventions—the rubber ball, which could bounce on the grass, and the lawn mower, which could keep the grass neat and finely cut—lawn tennis might not exist today.

Major Walter Wingfield is credited with having devised the earliest version of the game, which he called "Sphairistikē," the Greek word for "ball game." Since few people could pronounce this awkward name, it was quickly shortened to "Sticky" and finally abandoned in favor of the more straightforward title, Lawn Tennis. As it was not acceptable in mid-Victorian society for a gentleman to engage in "trade," Wingfield sold his game to the public indirectly through an agent, French & Co., in London. Since the game proved a tremendous success both at home and abroad, being played on vicarage lawns and on the grounds of stately homes, it wasn't long before established firms were selling similar games and sports equipment manufacturers were copying it.

A very rare Sphairistikē set, complete with a *Book of the Game* and an order book containing an impressive list of Wingfield's customers (culled mainly from the ranks of the aristocracy and the clergy), is just one of the myriad exhibits not to be missed at the Wimbledon Lawn Tennis Museum. Located next to the famed Centre Court, the site of the annual two-week-long Wimbledon Championships, this delightful museum makes excellent use of paintings, postcards, photographs, equipment, period costumes, and other assorted ephemera, to relate the often dramatic and fascinating social history of lawn tennis, a sport that began as a genteel game a little over a century ago, and which has developed into

INITIALLY, LAWN TENNIS WAS OFTEN ASSOCIATED WITH POLITE SOCIAL GATHERINGS SUCH AS THIS ONE REPRESENTING TEA AT THE VICARAGE, WHERE REFRESHMENTS IN THE FORM OF TEA AND CAKES WERE SERVED BETWEEN GAMES.

both an English institution and a multimillion-dollar international sporting event.

Thanks to the museum's sophisticated video and sound systems, the aura and excitement of some of this century's most famous matches may be seen and heard again, including tournaments played by such world-renowned champions as Chris Evert, Jimmy Connors, John McEnroe, and Martina Navratilova.

These dramatic replays are a far cry from the first Lawn Tennis Championship, which was held on the croquet lawns of the All England Club at Worple Road in Wimbledon in the summer of 1877. The finals of the Gentlemen's Singles Event were attended by a refined crowd of two hundred, fashionably dressed in top hats or white gowns. This early Wimbledon game was safe and dull, and had one chief aim: to hit the ball over the net. (Still, it's worth noting that the rules of 1877, with one or two modifications, are the same rules in use today.)

Oddly enough, it would take the warm personalities, powerful strokes, and tactical play of two sets of twins to transform lawn tennis into a spectator sport. The Renshaw twins, William and Ernest, dominated the tournaments throughout the 1880s, winning both doubles and singles matches repeatedly. After them came the Baddeley twins, Herbert and Wilfred, who were so alike that it was practically impossible to tell one from

A CHRONOLOGICAL HISTORY OF EVERY FACET OF TENNIS
IS COMPREHENSIVELY HIGHLIGHTED AT THE MUSEUM,
THROUGH COSTUMES,
SCALE MODELS, ORIGINAL MEMORABILIA,
CONTINUOUS AUDIO AND VIDEOTAPE LOOPS,
AND DETAILED WRITTEN DESCRIPTIONS.

the other—a daunting prospect for any opponents in the Gentlemen's Doubles!

By the early 1920s, lawn tennis had come into its own with a bevy of new and enthusiastic players who had both the talent and temperament needed to draw substantial crowds. It soon became clear that the Worple Road Ground could no longer accommodate the turnout, and the new Club moved to its present site. The new stadium could seat 11,000 spectators, with an additional 3,000 standing. These stands were built around the world-famous Centre Court, which was designed so that no shadow would appear upon it before seven in the evening.

Female emancipation also had a crucial impact on the development of lawn tennis as a women's sport. The museum's charming tableau of a lawn tennis party (a socially acceptable way for young men and women to meet) reveals the physical constraints Victorian women endured, hemmed in as they were by their steel-boned corsets, bustles, and layers of petticoats, as well as by a code of etiquette that decreed it was improper for a lady to play in public for fear of exposing her ankles! Keen to make a point about the hindrances of fashion, a number of female players persuaded a young man to play against them in full women's dress!

It wasn't until 1884 that a Ladies' Championship took place at Wimbledon, with Maud Watson as the winner. In 1905, the American player May Sutton became the first overseas champion. (Dublin's Fitzwilliam Club was actually the first to institute a Lawn Tennis Championship for women in 1879.)

Women's tennis was to undergo a major revolution in both dress and style during the 1920s, thanks in great measure to a charismatic young French woman, Suzanne Lenglen, who enjoyed a six-year reign at Wimbledon. Noted for having a fast, energetic style of play, as well as the headlines with her white two-piece suit and eyeshade. In 1929, Billie Tapscott from South Africa also made news by daring to play at Wimbledon without stockings, albeit on a back court. By 1933, Helen Jacobs would be wearing the first man-tailored shorts, leading the way for Gussie Moran to don lace-edged panties beneath her dress in 1949. With such daring fashion upstarts, it isn't altogether surprising that in 1962 a Wimbledon ruling was passed, decreeing that tennis dresses should be predominantly white.

The museum's encyclopedic approach also offers visitors the opportunity to see and understand the evolution of tennis rackets and balls and to appreciate how both have benefited from the introduction of strong and lightweight materials, including many from the aerospace industry. This technology has transformed tennis into a power game, where the ball can whiz by as fast as 140 miles per hour. However, some players argue that the harder serve and the aggressive volley have altered the game substantially, leaving less room for strategy and guile.

The Wimbledon Lawn Tennis Museum appeals to both tennis buffs and novices, thanks to its refreshingly informative approach in presenting the game's history and development, as well as to its extensive film library, which reveals the drama, skill, and intensity of this much-loved and avidly watched sport. If Wimbledon has emerged during the last hundred years as the world's most prestigious tennis tournament, this fascinating museum amply demonstrates why it merits such a stellar reputation.

THE CULMINATION OF EACH OF THE FIVE MAIN CHAMPIONSHIPS AT WIMBLEDON COMES WITH THE FINALS AND THE PRESENTATION OF TROPHIES SUCH AS THESE TO THE WINNING PLAYERS ON CENTRE COURT. THE SPLENDID TROPHIES SHOWN HERE ARE FOR MEN'S AND WOMEN'S SINGLES AND DOUBLES, AS WELL AS MIXED DOUBLES. MOST WERE MADE BETWEEN THE 1860S AND THE EARLY 1900S.

grace of a ballet dancer, she set off a storm by daring to shed her petticoat and corset in favor of a flimsy, short-sleeve, one-piece cotton mid-calf-length dress—an outfit that soon became the rage both on and off the court. At last, women had a tennis costume in which they could move!

Similarly, the invincible American Helen Wills, who became "Queen of Centre Court" in 1927, and then went on to win the Wimbledon Singles title eight times, made fashion

THIS EDWARDIAN MEN'S TENNIS LOCKER ROOM
IS A RECONSTRUCTION OF A
GENTLEMAN'S DRESSING ROOM AT THE
ALL ENGLAND CLUB
TOWARD THE END OF THE NINETEENTH CENTURY.

BIBLIOGRAPHY

———◆———

Ackerman, Diane.
A Natural History of Love.
New York: Random House, 1994.

Ades, Jane.
Dr. Johnson's House.
London: Dr. Johnson's House
Trustees, 1994.

Austen-Leigh, R. C.
A Guide to Eton College.
Eton: 1988.

Bryant, Julius.
The Iveagh Bequest, Kenwood.
London: London Historic House,
1993.

Burford, E. J.
A Short History of the Clink Prison.
London: Clink Prison, 1989.

**Dorey, Helen; and Thornton,
Peter.**
*A New Description of Sir John Soane's
Museum.*
London: Trustees of Sir John Soane's
Museum, 1990.

**Duffy, Stephen; Edge, David;
and Wenley, Robert.**
The Wallace Collection Guide.
London: Trustees of the Wallace
Collection, 1996.

Elsner, John; and Cardinal, Roger.
The Cultures of Collecting.
London: Reaktion Books Ltd, 1984.

Friedman, Joseph.
*Spencer House, Chronicle of a Great
London Mansion.*
London: Zwemmer, an imprint of
Philip Wilson Publishers, Ltd., 1993.

Gale, Matthew; Glennie, Sarah; Boden, Nicola; and Harrison, Michael.
Kettle's Yard and Its Artists.
Kettle's Yard: University of Cambridge, 1994.

Gee, Christina.
Keats House, Hampstead.
Norwich, U.K.: Jarold Publishing, 1990.

Goodman, Nigel.
Eton College.
Andover, U.K.: Pitkin Pictorials Ltd., 1976.

MacKenzie, Norman and Jeanne.
Dickens: A Life.
New York: Oxford University Press, 1979.

Mahon, Carol.
Duxford.
London: Imperial War Museum, 1992.

Morton, H. V.
In Search of London.
London: Methuen, 1988.

Ormond, Léonée and Richard.
Lord Leighton.
New York and London: Yale University Press, 1975.

Rothschild de, Mrs. James.
The Rothschilds at Waddesdon Manor.
London: William Collins Sons & Co., 1979.

Savill, Rosalind.
"This Palace of Genius, Fancy and Taste": The Wallace Collection, London.
Catalogue to the International Art and Antiques Fair at Harrods, 1993.

Schwartz, Selma.
Waddesdon Manor Guide.
Near Aylesbury, Buckinghamshire: Waddesdon Manor, 1996.

Scott, Rosemary.
Percival David Foundation of Chinese Art: A Guide to the Collection.
London: School of Oriental and African Studies, 1989.

Simon, Robin.
Lord Leighton and Leighton House: A Centenary Celebration.
London: Apollo Magazine, 1996.

Tames, Richard.
A Traveller's History of London.
Gloucestershire, U.K.: The Windrush Press, 1992.

Ward, Aileen.
John Keats: The Making of a Poet.
London: Secker & Warburg, 1963.

Waterfield, Giles.
Dulwich Picture Gallery.
Dulwich: Dulwich Picture Gallery, 1996.

Woodham-Smith, Cecil.
Florence Nightingale.
New York: McGraw-Hill Book Company, 1951.

INDEX